SO YOU THINK YOU'RE A
CHICAGO CUBS
FAN?

SO YOU THINK YOU'RE A CHICAGO CUBS FAN?

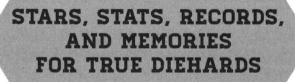

STARS, STATS, RECORDS,
AND MEMORIES
FOR TRUE DIEHARDS

SAM PATHY

SPORTS
PUBLISHING

Sports Publishing books may be purchased in bulk at special discounts for sales promotion, corporate gifts, fund-raising, or educational purposes. Special editions can also be created to specifications. For details, contact the Special Sales Department, Sports Publishing, 307 West 36th Street, 11th Floor, New York, NY 10018 or sportspubbooks@skyhorsepublishing.com.

Sports Publishing® is a registered trademark of Skyhorse Publishing, Inc.®, a Delaware corporation.

Visit our website at www.sportspubbooks.com.

10 9 8 7 6 5 4 3 2 1

Library of Congress Cataloging-in-Publication Data is available on file.

Cover design by Tom Lau
Cover photo credit: AP Images

ISBN: 978-1-68358-011-9
Ebook ISBN: 978-1-68358-012-6

Printed in the United States of America

To Kerry—the newest diehard Cubs fan
To the memory of Cubs fans who missed 2016

Contents

Introduction

The Cubs won the 2016 World Series! They fulfilled the dreams of longtime supporters, patient fans, and the city of Chicago. In fact, their championship year transcended sports, capturing the imagination of the whole nation.

The Cubs won the Series with style and verve. Unlikely heroes such as Kyle Schwarber, Javier Baez, and David Ross wrote storybook scripts like those on the big screen. The Cubs stormed back from a three-games-to-one deficit, winning Game 7 in extra innings after losing a four-run lead. The uninformed called these heroes and these comebacks "unCub-like," but that's not true. While the Cubs haven't won lately, they had won like this before. They dominated baseball back in the day.

The Chicago Cubs are baseball royalty, the prince in a world of kings and jesters. Never mind they spanned 108 years between elusive world championships. The Cubs were there (as the White Stockings) when the National League formed in 1876. And, although sportswriters called them the Colts (from 1890 to 1897) and the Orphans (from 1898 to 1902) before the Cubs, they're still the oldest one-city franchise in North America.

The Chicago Nationals were among baseball's best. The White Stockings won the inaugural National League title in 1876 and six of the first eleven. The Cubs were so good they didn't finish in last place until 1925, their 50th season. The

Cubs won 11 modern pennants from 1903 to 2016, the sixth most among the original 16 20th-century teams. And through 2016, they've won 523 more regular season games than they've lost: 10,711–10,188.

The Cubs franchise holds numerous records. They have the highest single-season winning percentage. They've scored the most runs in a single game and the most runs in an inning. The Cubs have the longest winning streak during a pennant drive and the longest stretch without being no-hit.

Franchise players include the first major leaguer to collect 3,000 hits, the first to record three no-hitters, the first African American to throw a no-hitter, the first to win back-to-back National League Most Valuable Player Awards, and the only one to hit more than 60 home runs in a season three times.

And the Chicago Cubs reside in Wrigley Field, a baseball cathedral, and an American treasure. The Friendly Confines is the last remnant of the ill-fated Federal League. It's the site of the only nine-inning double no-hit game in major-league history, the only two ballgames where both teams scored over 20 runs, Babe Ruth's disputed "Called Shot" home run, and the "Homer in the Gloamin'." It's the only ballpark left standing that Jackie Robinson played in.

When you discuss the Chicago Cubs, you discuss the history of Major League Baseball itself. The Chicago Nationals had their irons in the fire from day one; they helped develop and nurture the game. And after the young Cubs dramatic World Series win in 2016, they'll likely be among the darlings of baseball for the foreseeable future.

This book is more than just a trivia book—it provides the stories behind the answers. It shares the history of the Chicago Cubs, from the first days of the franchise to their recent World

Series triumph. So read the book, ponder the questions, and like Fergie Jenkins or Jake Arrieta before you, see how many of these questions you can "punch out."

This book is divided into four sections of questions organized by difficulty: easy (singles), medium (doubles), hard (triples), and expert (home runs), the ones for fans who know Kerry Wood's birthdate (June 16, 1977) and Travis Wood's hometown (Little Rock, Arkansas).

A hint? The questions in each section fall generally in chronological order.

To paraphrase the legendary Wrigley Field public address announcer, Pat Pieper: Attention! Attention please! Have your pencils and gray matter ready, and I will give you the questions for *So You Think You're a Chicago Cubs Fan*?

So toe the rubber and let's play ball!

SINGLES LEVEL

(Answers begin on page 5.)

This level includes the foundations of the franchise. It's basic Cubs history, covering many of the giants and the big highlights. There's lots of contemporary stuff too, including the guys who gave us the 2016 world championship. You should get through these without giving up a "big inning."

1. When did the Cubs win two straight World Series titles?
2. When was Wrigley Field built?
3. A batted ball stuck in the ivy is a ground-rule _____?
4. Who is the Cubs' all-time home-run leader?
5. What was the "Homer in the Gloamin'"?
6. Who was the first Cub to have his uniform number retired?
7. Who "clicked his heels" after home victories in 1969?
8. Who had the nickname "Sweet Swingin'"?
9. What happened on May 17, 1979?
10. What's so great about the 1984 season?
11. Who won the 1987 National League Most Valuable Player Award?
12. When did Wrigley Field get lights?
13. True or False: The wind usually blows out at Wrigley Field.
14. Which broadcaster celebrated each Cubs home run with a "Hey-hey"?
15. Whose favorite phrase was "Holy Cow!"?
16. Who won the 2005 National League batting title?
17. Name the manager who guided the Cubs to the 2007 and 2008 postseason?
18. Which players were involved in the Jake Arrieta trade?
19. The Cubs held six of baseball's top 41 prospects in 2014. Name at least three of them.
20. Who became the Cubs manager on November 2, 2014?

21. Name three of the six Cubs who homered in Game 3 of the 2015 NLDS?

22. Who led the Cubs in RBIs each year from 2013 to 2016?

23. Name at least three records or unusual statistics the Cubs set during the 2016 World Series.

24. In the 2016 World Series, who started the Cubs rally in the 10th inning of Game 7?

SINGLES LEVEL ANSWERS

1 The Chicago Nationals (White Stockings) won five National League titles in a seven-year span (1880–1882, 1885–1886). But the greatest dynasty belonged to the Cubs of 1906–1910. They won four pennants in five years, including back-to-back World Series titles in 1907 and 1908.

The Chicago Nationals (the Orphans) entered the 20th century on a 15-year pennant drought. In 1902, they hired veteran manager Frank Selee, who undertook a youth movement. Sportswriters called these young players the "Cubs." The soon-to-be-dynasty evolved piece by piece. Management brought in Joe Tinker at shortstop, Frank Chance at first base, Jimmy Slagle in center field, and Johnny Kling as full-time catcher. Johnny Evers settled in at second base. A bit later, Mordecai Brown, Ed Reulbach, Jack Pfiester, and Orval Overall strengthened the pitching corps. Harry Steinfeldt covered third base.

Frank Chance took over as player-manager in 1906 when Frank Selee retired for health reasons. The Cubs won a major-league record 116 games that year and met the White Sox in their first official World Series. The "Hitless Wonders" finished last in American League batting, but the South Siders outscored the Cubs 22–18, and won the final two games to take the series four games to two.

The undaunted Cubs won 107 games in 1907 and 99 more in 1908 to win back-to-back-to-back pennants. They overpowered Ty Cobb's Tigers to capture consecutive World Series, the first team to accomplish this feat. The Cubs pitchers dominated both series, losing only one game on the way to their two titles.

The Cubs won 104 games in 1909 but finished behind the Pirates. This happened in part because catcher Johnny Kling left the team to compete in and capture the 1909 world professional pool championship. Kling returned in 1910. That Cubs team won 104 games and grabbed another National League pennant. But they lost the World Series to the Philadelphia Athletics, four games to one. The A's outscored the Cubs, 35–15, and the dynasty ended.

The 1906–1910 Cubs finished 530–235, one of baseball's eminent teams. Fans called Frank Chance the "Peerless Leader," the Cubs' greatest manager this side of Cap Anson. The magician-like Mordecai "Three Finger" Brown tossed his way to an incomparable 127–44 record. And the famous double play combination of Tinker, Evers, and Chance found its way into baseball lore. Franklin Pierce Adams of the *New York Evening Mail* penned "Baseball's Sad Lexicon," his poem to the double-play trio that helped the Cubs vanquish their hated rivals, the New York baseball Giants.

> These are the saddest of possible words:
> "Tinker to Evers to Chance."
> Trio of bear cubs, and fleeter than birds,
> Tinker and Evers and Chance.
> Ruthlessly pricking our gonfalon bubble,
> Making a Giant hit into a double –
> Words that are heavy with nothing but trouble:
> "Tinker to Evers to Chance."

Joe Tinker, Johnny Evers, and Frank Chance—the great double-play combination. (National Baseball Hall of Fame Library, Cooperstown, NY)

Johnny Kling. (Photo Courtesy of the Library of Congress)

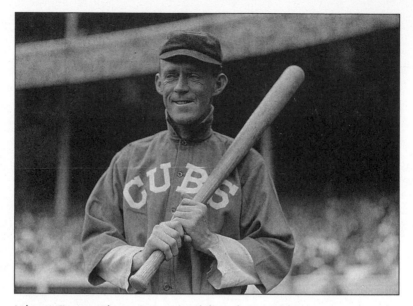

Johnny Evers. (Photo Courtesy of the Library of Congress)

2 Wrigley Field is linked both historically and emotionally with the Cubs. So it's ironic that the ballpark wasn't built for them.

Before the 1914 season the Federal League, an upstart minor league, declared themselves equal to the established National and American Leagues. The Chicago Federal League team owner, restaurateur Charlie Weeghman, hunted for a ballpark site. By forfeit Weeghman searched the city's less-developed North Side; the National League Cubs were a West Side institution, while the American League White Sox held court on the South Side. Weeghman leased a property at Addison and Sheffield. He opened Weeghman Park on April 23, 1914, a modest yet modern 14,000-seat steel and concrete ballpark.

The Federal League lasted just two seasons. The settlement with the establishment allowed two Federal League owners to buy into the National and American Leagues. One was Charlie Weeghman, and he purchased the Cubs. Before the 1916 season, he moved the Cubs from the rickety West Side Grounds to his two-year-old Weeghman Park on the North Side. The Cubs have called it home ever since.

The ballpark evolved rapidly. When Weeghman's restaurants hit hard times and he sold the team in 1918, Weeghman Park became Cubs Park. When interest in baseball skyrocketed after World War I, the team expanded Cubs Park. Workers cut the grandstand into thirds and separated and dragged the sections closer to Clark Street. Then they filled in the spaces like a giant jigsaw puzzle. The renovated park held 31,000 by 1923.

Fans filled the ballpark to capacity when the post-1925 Cubs started to win. Management double-decked the park (now called Wrigley Field). It happened just in time; the Cubs won National League pennants in 1929, 1932, 1935, and 1938. They set a major-league attendance record in 1929 that stood until after World War II.

Owner P. K. Wrigley renovated the ballpark twice more. The 1937–1938 renovation introduced a scoreboard-topped bleachers festooned with ivy on its brick walls. It turned a sturdy ballpark into the most handsome in the majors. It's also the greatest renovation project in major-league history. The look of the bleachers continues today, and the seats are still among the most coveted in baseball.

From the 1950s into the early 1970s, the Cubs renovated the ballpark again. They replaced most of the steel, concrete, and seats. These mundane updates kept the ballpark viable

Kansas City vs. Chicago—April 23, 1914. (Photo Courtesy of the Library of Congress)

into the 21st century. New restorations by the Ricketts family boosted Wrigley Field to an irresistible vibe of vintage yet modern, workaday yet beautiful.

3 Even casual baseball fans know Wrigley Field's ivy-covered walls. They first appeared after the 1937–1938 renovations. To make Wrigley Field more attractive and its outfield bleachers more utilitarian, management removed the old field-level bleachers and replaced them with raised bleachers, providing an attractive brick wall in front and storage space underneath. Bill Veeck Jr., or so he told it, admired the ivy-covered walls at a minor-league stadium and thought they'd spruce up renovated Wrigley Field.

When workers planted bittersweet ivy at the base of the brick wall in September 1937, no baseballs got lost in them. When they added dozens more Boston ivy sprigs in

April 1938, no baseballs lodged between them. It wasn't until August 13, 1942, that a sphere actually disappeared into the ivy. The Cubs' Bill Nicholson drove a ball that vanished against the right field wall. Before the Cardinals' Enos Slaughter found it, Nicholson had a two-run inside-the-park home run. A few years later, when the vines thickened even more, a new ground rule determined a lost ball equaled a double.

Outfielders now know to raise their arms when a ball sticks in the ivy. That way umpires call it a ground-rule double. But if the same outfielders comb the gnarled vines for the ball, play continues. That happened to the Cubs' Julio Zuleta on September 26, 2000. The Phillies' Kevin Jordan hit a line drive that Zuleta lost in the ivy. He panicked and ripped out leaves in a desperate attempt to uncover the ball. Jordan got a three-run inside-the-park home run. Zuleta never made that mistake again.

During the winters of 2013–2015, workers carefully pulled the ivy from the wall and set it down along the ground. They replaced portions of the outfield wall and tuck-pointed other areas. They then reaffixed the ivy to the wall. Grounds crew members claim some of those Boston ivy vines were the same ones planted back in 1938.

While only one major-league ballpark replicated Wrigley Field's outfield-filled ivy wall (Pittsburgh's Forbes Field), others added ivy to create hitting backgrounds. Even the White Sox's home park recently added hitting background ivy. If South Side fans, those North Side–hating, Wrigley Field–loathing denizens, tolerate it, then it's a marvelous thing.

4 Here are the Cubs top 20 all-time home-run leaders through the 2016 season:

PLAYER	HOME RUNS	YEARS WITH TEAM
20. *Rick Monday*	106	1972–1976
19. *Shawon Dunston*	107	1985–1996, 1997
18. *Jody Davis*	122	1981–1988
17. *Andy Pafko*	126	1943–1951
16. *Anthony Rizzo*	133	2012–date
15. *Leon Durham*	138	1981–1988
14. *Mark Grace*	148	1988–2000
13. *Andre Dawson*	174	1987–1992
12. *Derrek Lee*	179	2004–2010
11. *Alfonso Soriano*	181	2007–2013
10. *Hack Wilson*	190	1926–1931
9. *Hank Sauer*	198	1949–1955
8. *Bill Nicholson*	205	1939–1948
7. *Gabby Hartnett*	231	1922–1940
6. *Aramis Ramirez*	239	2003–2011
5. *Ryne Sandberg*	282	1982–1994, 1996–1997
4. *Ron Santo*	337	1960–1973
3. *Billy Williams*	392	1959–1974
2. *Ernie Banks*	512	1953–1971
1. *Sammy Sosa*	545	1992–2004

The skinny kid with the wildly aggressive swing developed into one of the game's most feared sluggers. No one but Sosa hit more than 60 home runs three different seasons (66 in 1998, 63 in 1999, and 64 in 2001). He hit more than 20 percent of the 60 longest home runs in Wrigley Field history.

Sosa and Mark McGwire enthralled the nation when they battled for the 1998 National League home-run title. Sosa's meteor-like 61st and 62nd home runs on September 13 led to three curtain calls and a near riot on Waveland Avenue. Later that month, Cubs fans celebrated Sammy Sosa Day. It foreshadowed Sosa's easy win in the 1998 National League Most Valuable Player Award voting.

But Sosa's baseball world began to fracture. Umpires caught him using a corked bat in 2003. He feuded all year with teammates and manager Dusty Baker. The final straw occurred during the final home game of the 2004 season. Sosa arrived late to the park, left early, and lied about it to management. The Cubs unceremoniously traded him soon after.

Sosa retired under the suspicion of using performance-enhancing drugs. He left a confusing and still-evolving legacy for Cubs fans. And like suspected users McGwire and Barry Bonds, Sosa's fallen short of enshrinement at Cooperstown.

5 The Cubs have hit over 6,550 home runs at Wrigley Field. Gabby Hartnett slugged the most important and the most dynamic on September 28, 1938.

The 1938 Cubs were pennant favorites. Their lineup overflowed with stars like Billy Herman, Stan Hack, and newcomer Dizzy Dean. But when they found themselves in third place on July 20, 5½ games behind the Pirates, P. K. Wrigley fired manager Charlie Grimm and replaced him with catcher Gabby Hartnett. Could player-manager Hartnett ignite the team to a pennant, just as Grimm did when he replaced Rogers Hornsby in 1932?

The Cubs trailed the Pirates by seven games on September 3. Beginning that day, the North Siders tore through a 17–3–1 streak to close to within 1½ games of the Pirates. On September 27, the teams began a three-game series in Wrigley Field, the outcome clarifying the pennant race. The Cubs won that day, 2–1. Now they trailed by only a half-game.

The September 28 battle ebbed and flowed, and the Pirates led 5–3 in the bottom of the eighth inning. A single by Ripper Collins, a double by Tony Lazzeri, and walks to Billy Jurges and Stan Hack got the Cubs to within a run, bases loaded, and still no outs. Billy Herman's single scored Jurges, but Paul Waner nailed pinch-runner Joe Marty at the plate. Frank Demaree tapped into an inning-ending double play. The teams were tied going into the ninth inning.

The clock read 5:30 p.m., just seven minutes before sunset. The umpires agreed the ninth inning would be the last. If the game ended in a tie, the teams would replay it the next day as part of a doubleheader.

Charlie Root set the Pirates down in the top of the ninth inning. Pirates relief ace Mace Brown easily retired the first two Cubs: Phil Cavarretta and Carl Reynolds. That put it in the hands of Hartnett. Brown snuck two knee-high fastballs past Gabby, but Hartnett rifled Brown's next pitch into the back of the left field bleachers. As he rounded the bases, players and fans spilled out on the darkening field. Hartnett fought his way through the jubilant mob to the safety of the clubhouse.

The miraculous home run did not win the pennant for the Cubs, but it catapulted them past the demoralized Pirates (the Cubs won the next day, 10–1). The Cubs clinched the pennant two days later in St. Louis. And even though the Yankees swept the World Series, the "Homer in the Gloamin'" became a touch point in club history. Writers and fans habitually compared later victories (and on-field celebrations) to the incomparable one witnessed by 34,465 frenzied fans on September 28, 1938.

Some hindsight on the eighth inning—if Waner had not thrown out Marty at the plate, if Demaree had not hit into a double play, the Cubs would not have batted in the bottom of the ninth inning. Hartnett's heroics would never have happened. Baseball is a game of inches. That's one reason it permeates our imagination.

(Hartnett's home run became known as the "Homer in the Gloamin'" based on a popular 1911 song, "Roamin' in the Gloamin'.")

6 When Ernie Banks slashed his first batting practice swing at Wrigley Field on September 14, 1953, he scorched the ball into the left field bleachers. The blast foretold great things for the rookie, who had recently toiled for the Kansas City Monarchs of the Negro Leagues.

Banks became an instant star. He sliced 44 home runs and drove in 117 RBIs in 1955, rare for a shortstop. He used his patented quick hands and powerful wrists to stroke 47 home runs in 1958 and 45 more in 1959. Add OPS numbers of .980 and .970, and Banks won back-to-back National League Most Valuable Player Awards. That had never happened before. He also became the first MVP Award winner from a team with a losing record. Heady stuff for a shortstop.

Ernie led the National League in games played six times. Banks played in 424 straight games to start his major-league career. When he returned from the hand infection that had felled him, he launched another 717-game streak from August 28, 1956, to June 22, 1961. This time an ankle injury derailed him. To protect his ankle he moved to first base, where he ended his career. In 19 seasons Banks played 1,125 games at shortstop, 1,259 at first base.

Age and injuries slowed down Banks, but the "Cub Power" era rejuvenated him one last time. He hit 32 home runs in 1968. The next year he drove in 106 runs. Banks clubbed his 500th home run on May 12, 1970. Stymied by bad knees, he got into just 72 games that year. He hit .193 in 1971 and retired after the season.

The 11-time All-Star hit 512 home runs and received well-earned recognition after his playing days. Sportswriters elected him to the National Baseball Hall of Fame in 1977. On August 22, 1982, the Cubs made Banks's uniform number 14 the first ever retired by the team. They erected a statue of Banks outside Wrigley Field and unveiled it on Opening Day 2008.

Banks's on-field excellence buoyed the Cubs through lean years. But his infectious personality and love for the game burned as strong. Banks coined the term "Friendly Confines" for his favorite ballpark. He exhorted teammates with his famous phrase, "Let's play two," even in the dog days of summer. Banks is the team's greatest player, its greatest figure, and the only one called "Mr. Cub."

Here are the Cubs' retired numbers as of 2017:

- Ernie Banks's number 14—August 22, 1982—flag on left field foul pole
- Billy Williams's number 26—August 13, 1987—flag on right field foul pole
- Ron Santo's number 10—September 28, 2003—flag on left field foul pole
- Ryne Sandberg's number 23—August 28, 2005—flag on right field foul pole

- Fergie Jenkins's number 31—May 3, 2009—flag on left field foul pole
- Greg Maddux's number 31—May 3, 2009—flag on right field foul pole

7 Ron Santo excelled at baseball and football at Seattle's Franklin High School. When the scouts paid a visit, Santo had his pick of either sport. Luckily he chose baseball. Every major-league team offered him a contract, but he signed with the Cubs. Santo admired Ernie Banks. And he felt he could get to the majors with the Cubs faster than with any other team.

Santo began at Double-A San Antonio in 1959 and hit .327. On June 24, 1960, Santo made his major-league debut at Forbes Field in Pittsburgh. Playing both ends of a doubleheader, the third baseman went 3-for-7, driving in five runs.

In 1962 Santo regressed; he hit just .227. But Santo kept a big secret. In early 1959, doctors diagnosed him with juvenile diabetes. Santo told virtually no one, lest they coddle him or worse, prejudge him. He started an insulin regimen but had difficulty getting used to it. His low blood sugar episodes also affected his on-field performance.

When Santo finally regulated his disease, his baseball numbers soared. He stroked a .962 OPS in 1964 and paced the league in triples, walks, and on-base percentage. He'd hit 30 or more home runs from 1964 to 1967 and drive in 94 or more runs from 1963 to 1970. He played in nine All-Star Games and earned five Gold Gloves. Santo became one of the league's most dominant players.

Santo acquired his soon-to-be-infamous calling card on June 22, 1969. In the bottom of the ninth inning, Jim Hickman walloped a home run for an improbable win. The Wrigley

Field crowd went wild. One Cub went over the top. As Santo trotted to the clubhouse in the left field corner, he jumped and clicked his heels. He did it again and again.

Santo continued the celebration after each home victory. Wrigley denizens loved it. As the wins piled up, so did Santo's clicks. But then the wins stopped. The Cubs collapsed, going from eight games in front of the Mets to eight games behind in just six weeks. Before the season ended, Santo stopped clicking.

The Cubs never won during Santo's career, and after the 1973 season they traded him to the White Sox. Santo played one dreadful year on the South Side and retired after the 1974 season.

Santo stayed away from the game. He opened a pizza parlor in 1962, eventually franchised the business, and even sold his pizzas at Wrigley Field. He worked offseasons for an oil company and later co-owned an oil business. He dabbled in truck stops and chicken franchises. He didn't need baseball anymore.

But the old saying proved true—you can take the athlete away from the game, but never the game from the athlete. Santo joined on as a WGN radio color man in 1990. His malapropisms and discussions of his toupees shared airtime with exclamations of "YES!" and moans of dejection. Santo sounded 100 percent authentic, and the Cubs faithful adored him. He became arguably the most beloved Cubs fan of all time.

Santo's diabetes finally caught up to him. He fought through numerous surgeries and eventually lost parts of both legs to the disease. He died on December 5, 2010, just 70 years old. Santo never reached the National Baseball Hall of Fame during his lifetime, but entered posthumously in 2012.

8 In the annals of Cubs history, no one played as consistently for so long a time as Billy Williams. And that swing—that beautiful left-handed swing. Fans named him "Sweet Swingin' Billy Williams." Old-timers still picture that swing as often as they like.

The Cubs signed the teenage Williams for $200 a month in 1956 and sent him to the Class-D club in Ponca City, Oklahoma. Williams hit just .235 in 13 games. To make things much more difficult, as an African American, he lived and ate with a family in town, since the hotels and restaurants restricted black customers.

Williams's early career wavered. He started 1959 in Double-A ball, but Billy's outfield defense dogged him. Hampered by self-doubt and homesickness, he developed stomach cramps. Billy had enough and left the team, and he returned to Whistler, Alabama. The Cubs sent Buck O'Neil, the former Negro League player and Cubs scout, to Whistler to talk with Billy. Buck convinced Williams that baseball was good for him, and convinced him that with work, Williams would succeed. Billy listened.

Williams returned to the game with a new perspective. He found out the pains came from a treatable ulcer. He developed his offensive skills and eliminated his defensive liabilities. After a short time at Triple-A, the Cubs promoted Billy to Chicago to finish the 1959 season.

Williams spent 1960 at Triple-A Houston and reached the big club again late in the 1960 season. The outfielder stuck with the Cubs in 1961. After hitting .278 with 25 home runs and 86 RBIs, Williams won the National League Rookie of the Year Award. All the bus travel, the degradation of segregation, the stomachaches, and the hard work paid off. Billy came to stay.

A model of consistency, Williams hit 20 or more home runs in 13 straight seasons. Outside of his first and last seasons, he never stroked fewer than 166 hits. In 1964, 1965, 1970, and 1972, he produced OPS numbers over .900. In 1965, he was the only major leaguer with a +.300 average, +200 hits, +100 runs, +30 home runs, and +100 RBIs.

Williams broke Stan Musial's 895 consecutive games played record on June 29, 1969. The Cubs celebrated Billy Williams Day that afternoon, and he received a plethora of gifts including a car, a boat, and a dog. He called it the greatest day of his baseball life. Williams set a then–National League record of 1,117 consecutive games played from September 22, 1963 to September 5, 1970.

Williams played his two best seasons in 1970 and 1972, but finished second in the National League Most Valuable Player Award voting both years to the Reds' Johnny Bench. Williams was disheartened, especially in 1972 when he won the National League batting title. But Bench's Reds won division titles each year. The Cubs finished second.

How consistent was Billy Williams? Over 14 full seasons on the Cubs he averaged a .296 batting average, 28 home runs, 96 RBIs, and a .869 OPS. And get this—he walked 1,045 times and struck out 1,046 over his career.

Billy Williams—Mr. Consistenc (National Baseball Hall of Fam Library, Cooperstown, NY)

9 With the wind howling out to the bleachers, pitcher Randy Lerch homered and the Phillies led the Cubs after just a half-inning, 7–0. The Cubs scored six first-inning runs of their own, the last on a triple by relief pitcher, Donnie Moore. Both starting pitchers lasted only ⅓ of an inning. It was going to be an interesting afternoon.

When the Phillies plated eight runs in the third inning and two more in the fourth, it looked like they'd pull away. That made sense to Cubs fans. The three-time National League East champions had overpowered the North Siders for years. Reasonable fans doubted the Cubs could come back from a 17–6 deficit.

But the Cubs did just that. They scored three runs in the fourth inning, seven in the fifth, and three more in the sixth. By then they trailed just 21–19. The longball drove this remarkable comeback. Steve Ontiveros and Jerry Martin blasted four-baggers. Dave Kingman slugged three towering shots of his own. And Bill Buckner launched a grand slam and drove in five of his eventual seven RBIs.

After the Phillies scored a run in the seventh inning and the Cubs clawed back with three runs in the eighth, the score was knotted at 22–22. The nearly 15,000 at Wrigley Field that day just shook their heads and smiled; both teams scored a week's worth of runs in a few hours.

The Phillies' Mike Schmidt, as he always seemed to do, poled a Bruce Sutter pitch into the left field bleachers for a 23–22, 10th-inning advantage. But there would be no more rallies or comebacks. Rawly Eastwick set the Cubs down in order in the bottom of the 10th for the win.

Here are more statistics and oddities from this mind-boggling game:

- The teams combined for 50 hits.
- No Phillies or Cubs starting-position players went hitless.
- The Phillies' Garry Maddox hit a home run and a double in the eight-run third inning.
- The Cubs struck out only four times.
- Of the 11 pitchers, only the Cubs' Ray Burris and the Phillies' Rawly Eastwick didn't give up a run.

The Cubs and Phillies put on a potent offensive display. Jack Brickhouse claimed he never saw anything like it in 40 years of broadcasting. While it's true that pitching wins ballgames, it's runs that put smiles on fans' faces.

10 The 1984 Cubs surprised Chicago like few teams in franchise history. General manager Dallas Green built the team two ways: He raided the Phillies of on-field and off-field talent, and traded aggressively during the season to stave off four decades of disappointment.

The irascible Green knew the Phillies well, and looted from the team he formerly managed. In December 1981 he landed Keith Moreland and Dickie Noles. In January 1982 he swapped shortstops—Ivan DeJesus to the Phillies for Larry Bowa. The Phillies threw in rookie infielder Ryne Sandberg. On March 27, 1984, Green went to the Phillies again and picked up Gary Matthews and Bob Dernier. They changed the Cubs immediately. Dernier's audacity on the field and Matthews's veteran leadership brought an expectation of success to the previously weak-kneed franchise. The outfielders joined more ex-Phillies: utility man Richie Hebner, and pitchers Dick Ruthven and Warren Brusstar.

Green didn't stop when the season began. On May 25, he peddled Bill Buckner to the Red Sox for pitcher Dennis Eckersley. On June 13, he swapped for Cleveland pitcher Rick Sutcliffe, who flourished immediately and pitched beyond belief. While going only 4–5 in Cleveland, he won 16 of 20 starts with the Cubs and finished the Chicago end of the season with a 16–1 record. Sutcliffe unanimously won the 1984 National League Cy Young Award.

That "throw-in" named Ryne Sandberg blossomed in 1984. The second baseman captured the spotlight during a nationally televised game against the Cardinals on June 23. Sandberg went 5-for-6 and drove in seven runs. He tied the game twice with home runs off Bruce Sutter: a solo ninth-inning blast and a two-run bomb in the 10th inning.

The Cubs won the contest dubbed "The Sandberg Game," 12–11, one that demarcated the old Cubs and the new confident Cubs. It also made Sandberg a star. He hit a slash line of .314/.367/.520. Add his offensive might to his Gold Glove defense and he walked away with the 1984 National League Most Valuable Player Award.

These first-rate Cubs motored into the playoffs. They clinched the National League East on September 24 in Pittsburgh, as thousands celebrated outside Wrigley Field. A week later, the Cubs played their first postseason game in 39 years. After Sutcliffe set the Padres down in the first inning, Dernier and Matthews homered. Matthews homered again, as did Ron Cey. Even Sutcliffe joined the rout and hammered a Sheffield Avenue drive in the third inning. The final record-filled score was 13–0, the most lopsided postseason win to date in major-league history.

After the Cubs won Game 2 at Wrigley Field, the teams went to San Diego. The Padres defied logic, swept the Cubs, and won the National League pennant.

Even with the playoff loss, it's impossible to underestimate the importance of 1984. After 39 years the Cubs finally won something. Nearly four decades of schlepping along, of falling behind, of accepting fate, had ended. The team also shattered their all-time attendance record by nearly 400,000 fans. From then on fans came to Wrigley Field like never before. The immediate area around the park—Wrigleyville—landed as a major destination for fans, too. Nearby bars and restaurants sprouted up in record numbers, filled before and after games, and even when there weren't games. The 1984 season changed everything.

11 Seldom does a team get a three-time All-Star and six-time Gold Glove winner dropped into its lap. But that happened to the Cubs in the spring of 1987.

Andre Dawson's knees wore down after a decade on the concrete-like artificial surface at Montreal's Olympic Stadium. He wanted to play half his games on real grass. Dawson and the Cubs were logical suitors because as an Expo, he hit a substantial .346 at Wrigley Field. Dawson offered his services and let the Cubs determine the contract. The Cubs offered one year at $700,000 with incentives. They low-balled Dawson, but he accepted anyway.

Dawson blasted a home run in his second game as a Cub, and never stopped hitting. He hit for the cycle on April 29, going 5-for-5 in an 8–4 win over the Giants. He homered on three consecutive days in early May to sweep the Padres. He scorched the Padres again on July 6 with two more pokes, the latter bouncing onto a second-story porch across Waveland Avenue. He produced an electric first half of the season: 24 home runs and 74 RBIs.

Dawson continued to pound the baseball in the second half. He homered in the third, fifth, and seventh innings on August 1, driving in all the runs for a 5–3 win over the Phillies. Three days later, he went deep in the 11th inning to beat the Pirates. But Dawson saved his best for last. In the season's home finale, Dawson came to bat in the eighth inning. After an enormous ovation from his rabid fans, he deposited a Bill Dawley changeup onto Waveland Avenue. As he rounded the bases fans chanted, "MVP! MVP!"

Dawson stung 49 home runs and 137 RBIs, both league highs. He won the 1987 National League Most Valuable Player Award, the first ever for a player on a last place team. Dawson batted 621 times, stole 11 bases, and won a Gold Glove—his knees held out on the soft Wrigley Field outfield.

Andre Dawson played six years in Chicago. And although he never replicated his amazing 1987 season, he hammered 179 home runs and an .834 OPS. Adoring Cubs fans loved the "Hawk." And it's safe to say Dawson loved Cubs fans, and Wrigley Field, too.

12 During the depths of the Great Depression in 1934, 10 of 16 major-league teams failed to draw 400,000 fans. As a life-saving experiment, the 1935 Reds played seven home night games. It worked. The Reds attracted nearly 20,000 fans per night contest and doubled their season attendance to 450,000.

As the Depression lingered, more teams bought artificial lighting. The Dodgers added it in 1938, the A's, Indians, and White Sox in 1939. Eleven of the 16 major-league teams played some home night games by 1941. These teams saw large attendance boosts, the most dramatic being the St. Louis Browns. The soporific Browns attracted just over 100,000 fans for the *entire* 1939 season. Their first four night games in 1940 drew more than 55,000.

Many curious Cubs officials attended Comiskey Park's first night game. They also saw the attendance upticks. So in late 1941, the team purchased the hardware—165 tons of steel, over 35,000 feet of copper wire, and light reflectors—to equip Wrigley Field for night games. But on December 7, 1941, Japan attacked Pearl Harbor, and the country entered World War II. P. K. Wrigley donated the precious materials to the war effort.

By 1948, the Braves, Yankees, Red Sox, and Tigers added lights for night baseball. Only the Cubs played all day games, and P. K. Wrigley hardened against lights. He called them an artificial stimulant that diminished over time. Even when he died in 1977, The Friendly Confines lacked artificial lighting.

The Tribune Company purchased the Cubs in 1981. They bought the team in part to guarantee programming of Cubs baseball for their own WGN television station. While day baseball brought in substantial revenues, night baseball brought even more. The Cubs played coy but couldn't hide their long-term intentions—lights and night games at Wrigley Field.

The Wrigleyville neighbors quickly organized. They presented their plight as the little man against the mammoth corporation. By August 1983 the Illinois House, the Senate, and the Chicago City Council agreed and passed laws that prohibited night games at Wrigley Field. The Cubs talked to Schaumburg, a Chicago suburb, as a possible relocation site. But the team wasn't going anywhere.

During the process something happened—the Cubs got good. They snared the National League East in 1984 and played postseason baseball. But since they couldn't host night games, the networks lost millions in revenue. The ABC network, which televised the 1985 World Series, mandated that all games be played at night. It would force Cubs "home" World Series games to Comiskey Park or worse, St. Louis. It meant potential lost playoff revenue to Chicago and Illinois. So soon after, the State Senate reversed course and allowed lights again at the ballpark.

The lights issue turned dramatically during 1987 as public sentiment sided with the team. The Chicago City Council repealed the lights ban, spurred on by the offer of the 1990 All-Star Game (and its financial windfall). The Cubs resurrected their electronic blueprints, mothballed since 1985.

The team played their first night game on August 8, 1988. But the "day-only" gods fought back; a fourth-inning rainstorm cancelled the game. The following night, August 9, became the first official night game. The Cubs beat the Mets, 6–4, and nearly 50 years of the lights debate flickered into oblivion.

13 Since wrecking balls razed San Francisco's Candlestick Park (of the infamous swirling gusts), wind affects Wrigley Field more than any other major-league ballpark. Three factors account for variations in wind speed and direction at the Cubs' home: Wrigley's proximity to Lake Michigan (less than a mile away), its midwestern climate, and its relatively squat height and open design that allows wind onto the field and into the stands.

Statistics published the last few decades consistently show that wind at Wrigley Field blew in more than it blew out: 50 percent to 30 percent. The stereotype of Wrigley Field as a hitter's paradise is wrong-headed. Southwest winds produce slugfests, but more often winds off the lake hold down scores.

Here's the average wind direction and speed each month at Wrigley Field:

- April—Northeast at 12 m.p.h.
- May—Northeast at 11 m.p.h.
- June—Northeast at 9 m.p.h.
- July—Southwest at 9 m.p.h.
- August—Southwest at 8 m.p.h.
- September—South at 9 m.p.h.
- October—South at 10 m.p.h.[1]

The wind generally blows in the first half of the season. It generally blows out the second half. But exceptions exist. That's why anxious players check the flags when they arrive at the park, many while still inside the team bus or in their cars. On days with variable or cross winds, players check the flags between pitches, something exclusive to Wrigley Field.

Early-season winds come off the lake. In the summer, the wind blows towards the lake. That's why games in April or May can be downright frigid. It also means that Chicagoans must check the weather forecast or bring a wardrobe of clothes when going to Wrigley Field. It's not uncommon for the temperature to vary 20 degrees or more between the warmer suburbs and the cooler lakefront. Some days shorts suffice in Wheaton, while a parka feels better in Wrigleyville.

Speaking of strong winds—the only game cancelled at Wrigley Field due to wind occurred on June 7, 1917. Harsh gusts shook the park's roof the day before. When the gales persisted the next day, management postponed the game before it even started.

14 If it "played in Peoria," Jack Brickhouse probably covered it. He grew up there. By the time he turned eighteen years old, he had begun working its beats and walking its streets, bringing radio to the citizens of that Western Illinois town.

Jack moved to Chicago in 1940 to broadcast baseball on WGN Radio. He hit the big time in 1948 when he called Cubs and White Sox home games on fledgling WGN TV. The next year three Chicago stations televised Cubs games. But Brickhouse and WGN gained exclusive rights to baseball at Wrigley Field by 1952. North Side fans relished Brickhouse. The Cubs even piped in audio of his WGN telecasts to sections of the left field grandstand.

Even as he broadcasted Chicago baseball, Brickhouse continued his "man about town" assignments. He hosted talk and interview shows, covered political conventions, and televised basketball and wrestling. The workaholic Brickhouse frequently covered a doubleheader at Wrigley Field during the day, then headed to the studio or another venue to do a show at night.

Even as Jack grew older he seldom took a breather. He called Chicago Bears football games on radio from 1953 to 1976. And Brickhouse didn't ease his workload when the White Sox left WGN in 1968. He added Cubs road games to his traditional home game schedule, becoming a welcome presence to Cubs fans all season long.

On August 5, 1979, Brickhouse broadcast his 5,000th baseball game. Illinois governor Jim Thompson and Chicago mayor Jane Byrne shared proclamations at the day's on-field ceremony. Jack and his Cubs broadcasts reached over 550,000 fans in 1979, as high as they'd ever been. The audience ran the gamut from retirees, to housewives, to children who scampered home from school to catch the last inning or two from Wrigley Field.

Brickhouse's simple "Hey-hey" home-run call punctuated Chicago summers. Sometimes rendered in a near-yell when the longball really meant something, Brickhouse's celebratory call screeched from television speakers into homes and neighborhood taverns.

Brickhouse retired from Cubs baseball after the 1981 season. Harry Caray replaced him, and Caray's over-the-top persona and salesman-conscience spiel out-eclipsed Brickhouse in popularity. But Cubs fans heard 50 consecutive years of excellence from these two beloved mic-men. Their skill and likability made the Cubs as popular as they are today.

On February 18, 1998, Brickhouse fell ill as he prepared himself for Harry Caray's funeral. Instead of attending the mass, he called a doctor. A medical test discovered a nickelsized tumor on his brain. The surgery succeeded and Brickhouse visited the Cubs' television booth later that summer. But Jack suffered cardiac arrest and died on August 6. The Cubs affixed his "Hey-hey" home-run call on the outfield flagpoles. It's comforting to still see them every game, but mature fans would give anything to hear it hollered again out of their television sets.

15 If you don't know this answer you never heard him. His gravelly voice, his gregarious manner, and his never-ending sales pitches overwhelmed anyone in earshot. The "Holy Cow!" answer is the fun-loving Harry Caray, probably the most popular person, player or otherwise, associated with the Cubs the past 35 years.

Born Harry Carabina on March 1, 1914, he lost both parents before his ninth birthday and lived with his aunt in a rough St. Louis neighborhood. Caray's hardscrabble childhood produced an adult who craved attention, and one who could land on his feet, no matter the situation.

Caray started in radio, and as a foretaste of his career as a pitchman, he literally talked his way into a job with the St. Louis Cardinals in 1945. His life-of-the-party persona, his famous home-run call ("It could be . . . it might be . . . it is. Holy Cow!"), and his rampant homerism made him popular with Cardinals fans. But he left after the 1969 season (stories explaining why range from Caray canoodling with the boss's wife to Caray trying to manipulate who managed the team).

After just one year with Charlie Finley's A's, Harry hooked up with the White Sox. The haphazard South Side team held less appeal at the time than Oakland, but an incentive-laden contract and the chance to carve out a niche with an established franchise whisked Caray to the Windy City. White Sox fans immediately took the irrepressible Caray as their own. The combination of Caray's "fan in the booth" identity and dogged promotion helped save the franchise from oblivion.

Bill Veeck bought the White Sox in 1976 and convinced Caray to perform his image-clinching trademark song, "Take Me Out to the Ballgame" during the seventh-inning stretch. When Veeck sold the White Sox in 1981, and the new owners schemed to put games on paid television, Caray fled. He knew far fewer fans would watch him than would on free television. And with Jack Brickhouse set to retire after the season, Caray took a bold chance and called the Cubs.

The two parties reached a deal, and it shocked Chicago. The longtime Cardinals announcer and the present White Sox warbler headed to the rival Cubs. How would Cubs fans take him? Very well it turned out, as North Side fans fell for Caray, too. And Harry's timing was perfect. The WGN Superstation beamed the 1984 National League East champs across the continent, with Caray's ginormous glasses and fractured speech leading the show. Seventy-year-old Caray was more popular than ever before.

Caray's career eventually slowed. He suffered a stroke in 1987, and his abilities slowly eroded. Caray planned to team with his grandson Chip in 1998. But on Valentine's night, Caray suffered a heart attack and died four days later. The Cubs continued Caray's famous seventh-inning stretch, using guest singers. The concept proved a fit of genius and still continues in some fashion today.

Twenty-five years in St. Louis, 11 on the South Side, and 16 more at Wrigley Field . . . Harry Caray always landed on his feet. The brash-talking salesman and the "Mayor of Rush Street" brought goofy joy wherever he went. He was bigger than life, just like his statue today outside the Wrigley Field bleachers.

16 After the Cubs lost the heartbreaking 2003 National League Championship Series to the Marlins, the last thing Cubs fan coveted were Marlins ballplayers—especially ones who contributed to the crucial Game 6 debacle. Yet after the 2003 season, the Cubs traded for Derrek Lee. It was Lee's double that knotted the score at 3–3 in the eighth inning of that Game 6, before the Marlins buried the Cubs 8–3 and eventually advanced to and won the World Series.

In hindsight the deal made tremendous sense. The Cubs shipped minor leaguer Mike Nannini and first baseman Hee-Seop Choi to the Marlins for Lee. The lanky first baseman spent seven years with the Cubs, won two Gold Gloves, stroked 179 home runs, and compiled a fantastic .903 OPS.

Lee turned in his best season in 2005. He led the National League in many offensive categories: a .335 batting average, 199 hits, 50 doubles, 393 total bases, a .662 slugging average, and a 1.080 OPS. Lee won a Gold Glove, the Silver Slugger Award, played in the All-Star Game, and finished third for the National League Most Valuable Player Award.

Lee's character graded as high as his on-field skills. The word *class* comes to mind. And Cubs fans appreciated Lee for it. That showed at the 2014 Cubs Convention, where he received thunderous ovations on his first return since he left the Cubs in 2010. But that's understandable. Lee made an indelible mark on the North Side, even if he added to the unbearable misery of 2003.

17 Managing the Cubs is tough. Leading a high-profile team in a large market ramps up stress. Failing to win the team's first pennant in decades destroys self-confidence.

Look at Don Baylor and Dusty Baker. Both arrived in Chicago with good pedigrees. Baylor led the expansion Rockies to the postseason in just their third year (the quickest ever to that point). Baker won the National League Manager of the Year Award three times and guided the Giants to the 2002 National League pennant.

With the Cubs just two years removed from a 1998 postseason berth, Baylor's 2000 squad underwhelmed with a 65–97 record. The team rebounded in 2001 and finished

88–74, but wilted in September and lost a Wild Card berth. The 2002 Cubs did Baylor in. The beleaguered Boys in Blue lost nine straight games in May and management sacked Baylor and his substandard 34–49 record. Baylor spent just two and a half years with the Cubs. The experience chewed him up and swallowed him whole. He never managed in the majors again.

Baker followed Baylor in 2003 and led the Cubs to the National League Championship Series. But he died a little after that horrible seven-game series loss to the Marlins. The Cubs won 89 games in 2004 but failed to make the postseason. The Cubs backtracked and finished below .500 in 2005. Baker's 2006 team lost 96 games, the worst in the National League. Management fired him after the season, and Baker took two years off to regroup. Baker managed four teams: the Giants, Cubs, Reds, and Nationals. He won more games than he lost with everyone except the Cubs.

That nefarious Cubs managerial position then targeted Lou Piniella. The two-time American League Manager of the Year and the field boss of the 1990 world champion Reds started well. The 2007 and 2008 Cubs won National League Central titles. The 2008 team won 97 games, the most since 1945. But both clubs choked in the postseason, outscored a combined 33–11.

The 2009 Cubs regressed and the 2010 team completely imploded. Piniella even quit before the season ended, a second-rate 51–74 record to show for his efforts. The grizzled manager finished without a bitter diatribe, an off-handed blow to management, or a stack of bats heaved onto the field. Just the exhausted skipper in tears with this confession: "I didn't want it to end this way."[2]

Piniella's managerial career mirrored Baylor and Baker's, prominent men of their profession who arrived in Chicago with high hopes. But they left in shambles as they failed to bring a championship to the North Side.

18 The Cubs made some good trades over the years. How about the 1966 deal that brought Ferguson Jenkins from the Phillies? Or maybe getting Larry Bowa and little-known Ryne Sandberg for Ivan DeJesus? Don't forget Aramis Ramirez and Kenny Lofton from the Pirates for Jose Hernandez, Bobby Hill, and Matt Bruback. But perhaps the best trade of all occurred July 12, 2013. The Cubs sent pitcher Scott Feldman and reserve catcher Steve Clevenger to the Orioles for pitchers Jake Arrieta and Pedro Strop.

The Cubs signed Feldman as a free agent on November 27, 2012. But they didn't plan to keep him. They hoped Feldman would perform well enough to flip him at the 2013 trade deadline. And that's exactly what happened. Feldman went 7–6 with a 3.46 ERA. The Orioles noticed and wanted Feldman for their stretch drive.

At the same time, the Cubs saw potential in Jake Arrieta. The pitcher held promise but struggled. (In 2013 the Orioles sent him and his 7.23 ERA down to the minors.) The Cubs thought the Orioles had altered Arrieta's delivery and wrecked his mechanics. They'd just let him pitch.

The trade played out as one of the most lopsided in recent memory. Feldman went 5–6 in one year with Baltimore. Clevenger collected just 53 hits. Pedro Strop grew into the Cubs' top set-up man. And Arrieta dominated. He went 12–1 with a 0.75 ERA after the 2015 All-Star break, the best second-half ERA in major-league history. Arrieta won the 2015

National League Cy Young Award. Through the 2016 season he went 54–21 with the Cubs, won half their 2016 World Series wins, and even tossed two no-hitters.

The Cubs used this strategy again in 2014. They signed pitcher Jason Hammel before the season and he went 8–5 through early July. That's when they traded him and Jeff Samardzija to the A's and landed Addison Russell.

The Cubs had fleeced teams before, but Theo Epstein and Jed Hoyer's judicious "sign and swap" strategy worked to perfection, and worked more than once. They traded useful but expendable pieces for a Cy Young Award winner and a budding All-Star. They say baseball is a thinking man's game. The Cubs' brass wielded their intellect to drive them to the 2016 World Series, and beyond.

19 Here are six of the top 41 prospects in 2014 (that's 14.6 percent of the top 100 prospects):

- Number 5   Javier Baez
- Number 8   Kris Bryant
- Number 14   Addison Russell
- Number 28   Carl Edwards Jr.
- Number 36   Albert Almora
- Number 41   Jorge Soler[4]

All these prized prospects reached the Cubs by 2016. They all played in the 2016 World Series, where all except Edwards were still 24 years old or younger.

Jake Arrieta—fleeced from the Orioles. (National Baseball Hall of Fame Library, Cooperstown, NY)

The Cubs took Javier Baez in the first round (ninth pick) of the 2011 amateur draft. The first of the group to join the Cubs, Baez debuted on August 5, 2014. In 213 plate appearances he struck out 95 times and hit just .169. In 2016 Baez's average ballooned to .273 and he dropped his strikeout rate to under 25 percent. A valuable utility player, Baez played second base, third base, first base, shortstop, and left field. He broke out in the 2016 postseason, with timely hits and acrobatic defensive plays. He shared the 2016 National League Championship Series Most Valuable Player Award with Jon Lester.

The Cubs took Kris Bryant in the first round (second pick) of the 2013 amateur draft. Bryant played at the University of San Diego where he began an amazing personal winning-streak of sorts. In consecutive years he captured the Dick Howser Award for the college player of the year, the Minor League Player of the Year Award, the National League Rookie of the Year Award, and the National League Most Valuable Player of the Year Award. That's unprecedented and portends great things for the young third baseman. Cooperstown awaits Bryant.

Addison Russell came to the Cubs in the July 2014 trade that sent Jeff Samardzija and Jason Hammel to the A's. A Gold Glove–caliber shortstop, Russell showed pop in 2016 when he belted 21 home runs and knocked in 95 runs. He hit three home runs in the 2016 postseason, including drives in Game 4 and Game 5 of the NLCS, and a grand slam in Game 6 of the World Series.

A 48th-round draft pick in 2011 by the Rangers, Carl Edwards Jr. came to the Cubs in the 2013 trade-deadline deal that included Justin Grimm, Mike Olt, and Neil Ramirez for Matt Garza. After a September call-up in 2015, the long-shot Edwards enjoyed a fine 2016. The razor-thin right-hander appeared in 36 games and flashed a minuscule .0806 WHIP. Edwards pitched in eight postseason games and posted a 2.84 ERA.

The Cubs took Albert Almora in the first round (sixth pick) of the 2012 amateur draft. Almora debuted on June 7, 2016, and hit .277 in 122 at-bats for the 2016 Cubs. Almora went 0-for-10 in the 2016 postseason, but pinch-ran for Kyle Schwarber in the 10th inning of Game 7 of the World Series. He scored the lead run on Ben Zobrist's double.

The Cuban native Soler defected to Haiti in 2011, and the Cubs signed him to a nine-year contract in 2012. Soler debuted on August 27, 2014. The often-injured outfielder batted just 277 times in 2016 and came to the plate just five times in the World Series. On December 7, 2016, the Cubs traded Soler to the Kansas City Royals for closer Wade Davis.

20 The guy with the nerd-cool glasses knows how to manage. The eight years before he came along, the Devil Rays compiled just a .401 winning percentage. The next nine years the shoestring-budget Tampa Bay teams played to a .528 winning percentage. Under Joe Maddon they earned their only four postseason appearances and a trip to the 2008 World Series.

It's no wonder Theo Epstein and Jed Hoyer tracked down Joe Maddon in one of the most unusual interview venues in baseball history—an RV park along the Gulf of Mexico.

After the 2014 season, the Rays' general manager left for the Dodgers. Joe Maddon's contract allowed a two-week opt-out clause in such a case. Maddon took the option, his chance to be a free agent of sorts. During the process, Maddon and his wife planned to drive their RV from Tampa to their winter home in Southern California.

By protocol all major-league teams got wind of Maddon's opt-out. Many were interested. But only the Cubs went to the extraordinary length to interview him first. Epstein and Hoyer tracked Maddon down in route to California and scheduled the interview in an RV park in the Florida panhandle. Epstein

Joe Maddon—the unique leader of the World Champion Cubs. (Photo courtesy of Sue Skowronski)

and Hoyer arrived in jeans, Maddon dressed in shorts and a T-shirt. The three met on the beach, drank a few beers, and talked baseball until the sun set.[3]

The Maddons continued driving west the next day. Before long and someplace in New Mexico or Arizona, with the Cubs and Maddon's agent negotiating by phone, Maddon became the 54th manager of the Chicago Cubs.

The team introduced Maddon on November 3, 2014, at the Cubby Bear across from Wrigley Field. After the lively press conference, Maddon offered everyone in attendance a shot and a beer. The idiosyncratic courtship and Maddon's distinctive public debut set the fans and the press on a whirlwind flirtation with the Cubs' new leader. And Maddon's on-field success secured his spot among the greatest of Cubs managers, as mighty as Frank Chance, Charlie Grimm, even Cap Anson.

Joe Maddon is far more than just live bear cubs at spring training, exotic animals in the clubhouse, and onesie road trips. He's a unique leader, the psychological guru who generates the best in people, and allows them the opportunity to succeed. He develops young players shrewdly.

Maddon lives life as Theo Epstein and Jed Hoyer's mirror-image—men who think far beyond their peers. In Maddon's first two seasons, the Cubs won 200 games. That hadn't happened in over 100 years. His Cubs played in two consecutive National League Championship Series and then won the 2016 World Series.

Epstein's and Hoyer's romp to the Florida panhandle is a story for the ages. Maddon's Cubs are one for the ages, too. They won the team's first pennant in 71 years, and their first World Series in 108.

21 On October 12, 2015, the Cubs and the Cardinals met in the first postseason game at Wrigley Field since 2008. It was a perfect night for baseball—73 degrees with a 17-mile-per-hour gale toward center field. It was the perfect night for the longball.

The Cubs went deep three times in the first five innings. Kyle Schwarber pounded an opposite field home run in the second inning. Shortstop Starlin Castro tied the score at 2–2 with a wallop in the fourth. Kris Bryant and Anthony Rizzo went back-to-back in the fifth inning; Bryant's drive knocked in Jorge Soler while Rizzo's solo clout traveled 430 feet to the right field bleachers. The Cubs led, 5–2.

The North Siders weren't done. Soler knocked in Chris Coghlan with a sixth-inning blast. Dexter Fowler launched one in the eighth inning, a towering shot that cleared the small LED board in right field. The Cubs triumphed, 8–6 on six home runs, a major-league postseason record. They took control of the series, up three games to one.

The teams met the next day at Wrigley Field. The temperature dropped 15 degrees and the wind blew only half as strong. But that didn't stop the Cubs from delivering a knockout punch. Javier Baez smoked a three-run home run in the second inning. The Cubs led, 4–2. Anthony Rizzo cracked a solo shot in the sixth, giving the Cubs a 5–4 lead. Rookie Kyle Schwarber belted a seventh-inning blast deep into the night. When it finally came down it landed on top of the new right field scoreboard, a mammoth drive estimated at 438 feet. The next day management encased Schwarber's ball in glass atop the scoreboard, a monument to the young Cubs and their immense power.

The Cubs vanquished the Cardinals and altered the balance of power in the National League's Central Division. With players like Soler, Schwarber, Bryant, Rizzo, and Baez, a tremor shook the ground beneath Major League Baseball. These young Cubs did great things: Soler reached base his first nine times to break a major-league postseason record, and Schwarber slugged five home runs, the most by any Cub to date in a postseason career.

The Cubs lost to the Mets in the 2015 National League Championship Series. But you knew they'd make their mark before too long.

22 The Boston Red Sox drafted Anthony Rizzo right out of high school, in the sixth round of the 2007 amateur draft. The next spring doctors diagnosed the teenager with Hodgkin's lymphoma—cancer. Following six months of chemotherapy and recovery, Rizzo returned to the game.

After Red Sox assistant general manager Jed Hoyer left to take the general manager's job with the Padres, he traded

Anthony Rizzo—the best left-handed Cubs hitter since Billy Williams. (Photo courtesy of Sue Skowronski)

for Rizzo. The young first baseman played on the 2011 Padres but batted just .141. When Hoyer moved to the same position with the Cubs in October 2011, he again traded for Rizzo. Even though Rizzo struggled with cancer and failed his only major-league test, Hoyer recognized something special. It's that "something" that teammates and fans see today.

Anthony Rizzo is that near perfect player, the perfect teammate. He's competitive. He's clutch. And if television images can be trusted, he's caring. He's always one of the first to interact with teammates, to congratulate teammates, and to support teammates. He seems genuinely excited to be on the field, excited to be on the Cubs.

The Cubs finished 2014 in last for the fifth-straight year. They struggled, mere punching bags for the rest of the National League. On July 10, 2014, the Cubs visited the Reds and faced Aroldis Chapman. The big reliever with the 100+-mile-per-hour fastball threw tight to the Cubs' Nate Schierholtz. It played out like many on-field moments over the past five years—another team, another All-Star pushing the Cubs seemingly at will. Anthony Rizzo stood in the dugout and watched. Then that "something" kicked in. Rizzo gave Chapman verbal hell. Chapman struck out Schierholtz to end the inning. The big reliever blew off, literally waved off Rizzo's criticism with a sweep of his hand as he left the mound.

After Rizzo went to his defensive position at first base, he continued to jaw at Chapman, now in the Reds dugout. When other Reds joined the verbal confrontation, Rizzo threw down his hat and glove, strode toward the dugout, and challenged any Reds players to a physical confrontation. The benches cleared.

Nothing much physical came out of this typical baseball scuffle. But Rizzo's teammates got the message. They saw Rizzo go to the floor for them. They saw Rizzo challenge the whole Reds team. They saw Rizzo declare "enough was enough." That incident marked the end of the lethargic Cubs. Next year the Cubs won 97 games, and it would be the Reds, not the Cubs that shriveled under the competition. Jed Hoyer knew that would happen someday.

This Cubs team is Rizzo's team now. In his first four full years, Rizzo led the Cubs in RBIs (80, 78, 101, and 109). During that same period he cracked 118 runs, the most in the National League.

Jed Hoyer believed in Anthony Rizzo from day one. He believed in the 207th player chosen in that 2007 draft. He believed in the only player from the sixth round to play a full year of major-league baseball. Hoyer believed in Anthony Rizzo. And Rizzo led the Cubs as they surged to the 2016 World Series.

23 World Series Records:

- The Cubs became the first team since the 1960 Pirates to win a World Series while being shutout twice (Games 1 and 3).
- The Cubs' Game 2 lineup featured six players 24 years old or younger: Kris Bryant (24), Jorge Soler (24), Kyle Schwarber (24), Willson Contreras (23), Javier Baez (23), and Addison Russell (22). That had never happened before in World Series history.
- Kyle Schwarber became the first position player to go hitless during the season but get a hit during the World Series.
- Addison Russell drove in six RBIs in Game 6. That tied the record for most RBIs in a World Series game (Richardson 1960, Matsui 2009, and Pujols 2011).

- Kris Bryant and Anthony Rizzo were the first "three and four" hitters in the batting order to get seven combined hits in a World Series game (Game 6).
- Dexter Fowler stroked the first leadoff home run in a World Series Game 7.
- When David Ross homered in the sixth inning of Game 7, he extended his own record as the oldest catcher to homer in the postseason (39 years old). He hit a home run in Game 4 of the NLDS on October 11, 2016.
- Willson Contreras, David Ross, and Miguel Montero all had RBIs in Game 7. That's the first time three catchers from one team had RBIs in one World Series game.

Cubs Records:

- The Cubs played their latest date ever at Wrigley Field—October 30 for World Series Game 5.
- Dexter Fowler became the first African American to play for the Cubs in a World Series when he came to bat in Game 1 on October 25, 2016. Addison Russell, Jason Heyward, and Carl Edwards Jr. joined him later in the game.
- Kris Bryant and Dexter Fowler hit two home runs in the World Series. They're the first Cubs to hit two since Frank Demaree in 1935.
- Kris Bryant became the first Cub to hit home runs in consecutive World Series games (Games 5 and 6).
- Kris Bryant, Addison Russell, and Anthony Rizzo hit home runs in Game 6. That's the first three-home-run game in Cubs World Series history.

Unusual Statistics:

- The Cubs won the World Series for the first time in 108 years, and played in the World Series for the first time in 71 years.
- An incredible 39,466 days passed between the end of the 1908 World Series and the beginning of the 2016 World Series.
- The Cubs had played 11,309 ballgames since their last World Series game.
- The Cubs had used 1,275 players since the 1945 World Series.
- Ben Zobrist became the second player to start a World Series with back-to-back three-hit games in two consecutive years (in 2015 with the Royals and 2016 with the Cubs). Babe Ruth was the first to achieve this feat, in 1927 and 1928 with the Yankees.
- Jake Arrieta threw 5 2/3 innings of no-hit ball in Game 2, the pitcher to get closest to a World Series no-hitter since Jerry Koosman, who threw six innings of no-hit ball in 1969 (Game 2).
- The Cubs faced the minimum number of batters (27) in NLCS Game 6. This only happened once before in post-season history, during Don Larsen's perfect game in Game 5 of the 1956 World Series.
- Addison Russell became the second youngest player to hit a grand slam in World Series history (Mickey Mantle at 21 years old in 1953).
- Addison Russell and Javier Baez tied a World Series record when they became the second pair of teammates under age 24 to homer in a World Series (Fred Lynn and Dwight Evans of the 1975 Red Sox).

- The Cubs are just the sixth team in World Series history to come back from a three-games-to-one deficit. They became just the fourth team to do this and win Games 6 and 7 on the road (1958 Yankees, 1968 Tigers, and 1979 Pirates).

The 2016 Cubs added glorious phrases to their lexicon. Here are a few made famous during and immediately after the 2016 World Series:

- "1,300 pitches"—number of batting machine pitches Kyle Schwarber saw before the World Series.
- "Best tagger"—moniker given to Javier Baez for his defensive wizardry.
- "Eight-out relief appearance"—Aroldis Chapman's Game 5 relief work.
- "I'm an emotional wreck!"—Anthony Rizzo's comment to David Ross during Game 7.
- "'Magic' rain delay"—the 17-minute rain delay that turned the Cubs' fortunes in Game 7.
- "Chalk wall"—fan comments written on the walls outside Waveland and Sheffield Avenues.
- "5 million"—estimated number of fans who attended the World Series parade and rally.

24 The Cubs lost a 5–1 lead in the pivotal Game 7 of the 2016 World Series. They also let a 6–3 eighth-inning lead slip away. They lost momentum. And with the Cubs and the Indians tied, 6–6 after nine innings, a collapse seemed imminent. You don't win 103 games in the regular season, sport a 252-run differential, and expect to lose Game 7 after blowing a four-run lead. But the Cubs seemed destined to do just that. You could feel it. Their fans expected them to lose that game, and the series.

The rain that spit from the sky in the ninth inning intensified. Now it showered hard enough for the umpires to delay the game, for the grounds crew to tarp the field. Before the 10th inning, the teams reported to their respective clubhouses. But the Cubs' Jason Heyward gathered the team in an adjacent weight room. Heyward spoke to his disheartened teammates. He reminded them of their recent accomplishments. He reminded them that they were the best team in baseball. "We've overcome it before. We can do it again,"[5] said Heyward, and he implored his teammates to focus on the opportunities ahead, not the runs lost.

The rain delay lasted just 17 minutes. The Cubs came to bat in the 10th inning with a renewed vigor. Kyle Schwarber led off and laced a sharp single to right field. Rookie Albert Almora pinch-ran. Kris Bryant flied to deep center for an out. Almora hustled to second base after the catch. The Indians intentionally walked Anthony Rizzo. Ben Zobrist ran the count to 1–2, then drilled a Bryan Shaw pitch past third baseman Jose Ramirez. Almora scored the lead run, Rizzo to third, Zobrist to second with a double. The Indians intentionally walked Addison Russell. Miguel Montero slipped a single between short and third, and Rizzo scored the insurance run.

The Indians got back a run after two were out in their half of the 10th. Then lefty Mike Montgomery induced Michael Martinez to dink an infield hopper that third baseman Kris Bryant nestled and threw to Rizzo at first base. The Chicago Cubs *were* the champions of baseball. One hundred eight years of bitter defeat had ended!

Who started the Cubs' winning rally? Was it Schwarber? The first man to get on base in the 10th? The man with the .500 on-base percentage in the series after contributing no hits during the season? The man with the 1.178 postseason OPS, which trails only the great Ruth and Gehrig in all-time post-season OPS (minimum 50 at-bats)? Or was it Jason Heyward? The man who hit only .150 for the series? The man with the slim .300 World Series OPS? But the man who inspired the Cubs during the "magic" 17-minute rain delay? You decide. Either is correct!

With the cumulative effect of 108 consecutive years of ultimate disappointment, November 2, 2016, ended as the greatest day in the 141-year history of the Chicago Cubs.

2

DOUBLES LEVEL

(Answers begin on page 55.)

These delve a bit deeper. There are still questions about great Cubs and great teams, but most are a little older, a little fuzzier to the average fan. Watch out! The batters are starting to dig in on you.

1. Why was Mordecai Brown called "Three Finger"?
2. What was the "Double No-Hitter"?
3. What was the highest-scoring game in major-league history?
4. Which Cubs team before 2016 last won 100 games?
5. Who was the Cubs' greatest catcher?
6. Which pitcher won the most games in Cubs history?
7. Who is the best-known native Chicagoan to manage the Cubs?
8. Was there really a curse that kept the Cubs from winning the World Series?
9. Who won the 1952 National League Most Valuable Player Award?
10. Who was the last Cubs pitcher to lose at least 20 games in a season?
11. True or False—the Cubs have an all-time losing record against the Cardinals?
12. Why is Wrigley Field still standing? Give two reasons.
13. Who was the greatest Canadian-born Cub?
14. Who spent the most years as the Cubs' leadoff hitter?
15. Which Cubs brothers had the highest combined WARs?
16. Which Cub last won consecutive National League batting titles?
17. Name the greatest "Cubs killer."
18. Did playing all home day games back in the day hurt the Cubs?

19. What did Bill Buckner and Leon Durham have in common? Name two things.

20. Who won the home-run-hitting contest at the 1990 All-Star Game at Wrigley Field?

21. Who hit three home runs on Opening Day?

22. Which Cub had more hits, doubles, and sacrifices in the 1990s than any other major leaguer?

23. Who sang the worst rendition of "Take Me Out to the Ballgame"?

24. This future Cubs battery won Wrigley Field's 100th anniversary game on April 23, 2014.

DOUBLES LEVEL ANSWERS

1 Mordecai Brown was the first great Cubs pitcher of the 20th century. Nicknamed "Brownie" or "Miner" because he played for coal mining company baseball teams, he later answered to another moniker, "Three Finger." Five-year-old Mordecai shredded parts of two fingers in a machine accident on his family's Indiana farm. The tragedy boosted his eventual baseball career; losing half an index finger on his right hand allowed Brown to mesmerize with his curveball. The sinking spinning pitch cursed the opposition, who continually pounded balls into the ground.

Brown came to the Cubs from the Cardinals in 1904 and won 15 games that year and 18 more in 1905. He put it together in 1906 and grabbed 26 wins, the first of six consecutive 20 or more win seasons. During the Cubs 1906–1910 dynasty, Brown won 127 games, the most consistent pitcher on the staff. Without Brown there would have been no dynasty, no four pennants, and no back-to-back World Series wins.

Brown pitched big in the clutch. He won five World Series games (1906, 1907, two in 1908, and 1910), the most in franchise history. From 1904 to 1912, Brown went 7–7 against the New York Giants' legendary Christy Mathewson. During the Cubs-Giants one-game playoff in 1908, Brown came on in relief in the first inning. In front of a veritable mob at the Polo Grounds, he held the Giants at bay the rest of the way and beat Mathewson 4–2 to send the Cubs to their third straight World

Series. Brown that day pitched the most significant mound performance in Cubs history.

The Cubs released Brown in 1912 after a knee injury. He signed with the Reds, then jumped to the Federal League in 1914. The following year he played on the Chi-Feds and snared 17 wins for the Federal League champs.

The 39-year-old rejoined the Cubs in 1916, but pitched ineffectively. Brown hurled his final game during a Labor Day doubleheader against the Reds. His opponent? The great Christy Mathewson. In what would also be Mathewson's last game, both went the distance, pitching on little but past reputations. This time Mathewson won, his 373rd and final win. And though Brown and Mathewson gave up 18 runs between them, Chicago fans saw an unforgettable farewell from the two grizzled competitors.

Brown is one of the greatest all-time Cubs. He holds the team's modern record for lowest ERA (1.80), and leads the team since 1900 in complete games (206) and shutouts (48). He won 188 games, and easily served as the lynchpin of the great Cubs dynasty. The farm kid with the deformed hand did pretty well for himself. And Cubs history is much richer because of it.

Mordecai Brown owns the lowest ERA in modern Cubs history. (National Baseball Hall of Fame Library, Cooperstown, NY)

2 Jim "Hippo" Vaughn stood 6'4" and at his lightest weighed 215 pounds. He earned his name not by his size, but for his odd gait. Hippo won 20 or more games five times in a six-year period (1914–1919). He went 22–10 in 1918 with a 1.74 ERA, a 1.006 WHIP, and a 7.8 pitching WAR. He'd have won the National League Cy Young Award if it existed at the time. Vaughn's stellar season led the Cubs to the 1918 pennant. He won 178 games in his long career, and sits alone as the premier Cubs left-handed pitcher.

Vaughn's best known for his prominent role in the famed "double no-hitter" at Weeghman Park on May 2, 1917. Hippo Vaughn and the Reds' Fred Toney pitched no-hit games through nine innings. With one out in the 10th, the Reds' Larry Kopf lined a solid single to right field to end Vaughn's gem. After one out, Hal Chase drove a ball to center field, but Cy Williams muffed it, leaving Reds on first and third. Jim Thorpe batted next. The 1912 Olympic decathlon and pentathlon gold medalist (a swift runner) hit a slow roller in front of the mound. Vaughn charged the ball, realized he had no chance to throw out Thorpe, and flipped the ball to Art Wilson, the Cubs catcher. But Wilson dropped the errant throw as Kopf scored, and the Reds took a 1–0 lead. Toney retired the Cubs in order in the 10th inning to preserve his no-hitter.

Fans referred to this epic game as the "double no-hitter," and in most minds it fits that description. But in 1991 Major League Baseball redefined a no-hitter. The new interpretation dictated a no-hitter must be at least nine innings long and the pitcher(s) must complete the game as a no-hitter. The new definition took away Vaughn's gem and credited him with only a two-hitter.

Toney and Vaughn's paths crossed that cold day in Chicago. They gave baseball the best-pitched game in major-league history, the double no-hitter—no matter how it's defined today.

Hippo Vaughn. (Photo Courtesy of the Library of Congress)

3 The Cubs hold many major-league scoring records. They plated the most runs in a single game, a 36–7 win (as the Colts) on June 29, 1897, against the Louisville Colonels. They scored the most runs in an inning, 18 of them (as the White Stockings) on September 6, 1883, against the Detroit Wolverines. They had plated over 96,000 runs as of the end of the 2016 season.

The Cubs also won the highest-scoring game in major-league history when they outlasted the Phillies, 26–23 at Cubs Park on August 25, 1922. The slugfest broke or tied numerous records. The teams combined for 49 runs, besting the old mark of 43. The Cubs tied two modern records when they scored 14 runs on 11 hits in the fourth inning. Marty Callaghan tied a record when he batted three times in that fourth inning. The Phillies' Russell Wrightstone and Frank Parkinson batted eight times in a nine-inning game, the first players to do this in the 20th century.

The 26–23 score never should have ballooned like it did. The teams combined for nine errors (21 unearned runs). The Cubs also let the Phillies back into the game when they sent two rookie hurlers to protect a 26–9 lead.

Nineteen-year-old Uel Eubanks started the eighth inning. The neophyte had pitched in only one previous major-league game, and the Phillies plastered him. They scored eight runs in only 2/3 of an inning. The shell-shocked Eubanks never pitched for the Cubs again, but wallowed six more years in the low minors for teams like the Greenville Staplers and the San Angelo Sheep Herders.

Ed Morris replaced Eubanks. The Phillies scored four runs off Morris in 1/3 of an inning. Morris appeared in 5 games with the 1922 Cubs but didn't resurface in the majors for six years. He won 19 games for the 1928 Red Sox, the first of four seasons with Boston. On February 29, 1932, Morris's friends threw him a going-away fish dinner before spring training. Things got out of hand and someone stabbed Morris in the chest. He died three days later at just 32 years old.

The final oddities about the highest-scoring game in history? The teams stroked only three home runs (the Cubs' Hack Miller hit two, teammate Bob O'Farrell hit one). The game finished in 3:01, an average game time in 2017.

4 The next great Cubs team after the 1906–1910 dynasty won a pennant every three years. They captured National League titles in 1929, 1932, 1935, and 1938. The four squads averaged 94 wins a season, but only the 1935 team won 100 games, going 100–54. They reeled off 21 straight wins in September, the greatest stretch run in major-league history.

Most writers in a 1935 preseason poll picked the Cardinals or Giants to win the National League. The Giants led most of the season, with the Cardinals and Cubs in hot pursuit. On September 3, the Cardinals pulled ahead of the Giants by two games, with the Cubs trailing by 2½ games. That's when the Cubs caught fire. Starting on September 4 they beat the Phillies four straight. Then they took four from the Braves, four from the Dodgers, four from the Giants, and two from the Pirates.

The Cubs played their final five games in St. Louis. They sported an 18-game winning streak and led the Cardinals by three games. Phil Cavarretta poked a home run and Lon Warneke two-hit the Redbirds in a 1–0 opening win. Their magic number dropped to two. The next day the Cubs swept the Cardinals, 6–2 and 5–3, to clinch the pennant and extend the streak to 21 games.

The illustrious Cubs outscored their opponents during the streak 137–50 and eagerly awaited the Tigers in the World Series. Things looked good after the first two games; the teams split in Detroit and Tigers slugger Hank Greenberg left the series with a broken wrist. But Game 3 got away from the Cubs. Umpires tossed Woody English, Charlie Grimm, and Tuck Stainback for bench jockeying. Bill Lee and Lon Warneke couldn't hold an eighth-inning lead. And third baseman Fred Lindstrom committed a costly 11th-inning error that led to the Tigers' winning run. The Boys from Motown took off from there and grabbed the series in six games.

How lucky Cubs fans had been. Two pennants preceded this wonderful season, and one more followed three years later. Fans admired stars like 1935 MVP Award winner Gabby

Hartnett and the two 20-game winners, Warneke and Bill Lee. A pennant every three years? Cubs fans today would still take it, and savor it to no end.

5 Charles Leo Hartnett had leadership burned into his bones, being the oldest of 14 children. He grew up in Western Massachusetts and worked early on at a rubber business. He played amateur baseball and signed a $1,900 contract with the Cubs. Hartnett joined the team in 1922. A sportswriter nicknamed him "Gabby" when he spoke very little as a rookie. But Hartnett outgrew his shyness and lived up to his sobriquet.

Hartnett established himself as an elite catcher, both on offense and defense. Hartnett took over for the injured Bob O'Farrell in 1925 and pounded 24 home runs, the most to that point by a backstop. His .354 batting average in 1937 held as a catchers' best until Mike Piazza hit .362 in 1997. Hall of Fame manager Joe McCarthy said this about his arm: "Gabby was the greatest throwing catcher that ever gunned a ball to second base. He threw a ball that had the speed of lightning, but was as light as a feather."[6]

Hartnett figured prominently in the Cubs' success during the Depression. He won the National League Most Valuable Player Award in 1935 when he batted .344/.404/.545, stroked 13 home runs, and scored a 5.0 WAR. He finished second in the 1937 MVP Award vote (.354/.424/.548). The next year Hartnett batted only 353 times but still finished 10th. Hartnett played in the first six All-Star Games (1933–1938). He managed the Cubs from July 1938 through 1940.

Hartnett owned a bowling alley and sports equipment store after he retired. He excelled at bowling and won scores of tournaments in the Chicago area. He entered the National

Baseball Hall of Fame in 1955. Hartnett died on his 72nd birthday, December 20, 1972, after a series of ailments.

Most recognize Hartnett as the National League's best catcher before Johnny Bench. The longtime Chicago sportswriter and Major League Baseball's first official historian, Jerome Holtzman, called Hartnett the greatest Cub of all time, better than Ernie Banks. Both men played 19 exceptional years, but Holtzman valued Hartnett's leadership qualities. "He was constantly talking it up, encouraging, exhorting, sometimes admonishing his teammates to greater effort."[7]

Hartnett hit the famous "Homer in the Gloamin,'" that late-season four-bagger that put the Cubs in first place in the 1938 pennant race. Hartnett frequently called that dramatic drive the greatest thrill of his life. Any Cubs fan who saw it in-person on September 28, 1938, would agree. Hartnett's home run ranks as the single greatest event in Cubs history, one more than 140 years in the making.

6 The 19th-century marvels who won over 40 games in a season: Albert Spaulding, Larry Corcoran, John Clarkson, and Bill Hutchison—don't lead the pack. Neither do Clark Griffith, Mordecai Brown, and Fergie Jenkins, the six-time 20-game winners. The man with the most Cubs victories only once won more than 20 games in a season. And only a little more than half of his 632 appearances came as a starter. He played 16 years on the North Side and won 201 games through longevity, not necessarily through greatness. The pitcher is Charlie Root.

Charlie Root's major-league career began in 1923 with a short stint on the St. Louis Browns. He went 0–4 that year, hardly a prediction of great things ahead. Root moved to the Cubs' Los Angeles farm team and excelled, going 21–16 in 1924, and 25–13 in 1925. Root joined the Cubs in 1926 and won 18 games. The next year he chalked up 26 more.

Root gave consistency to a Cubs staff with lots of turnover. Big-league arms like Guy Bush, Sheriff Blake, Pat Malone, Lon Warneke, Bill Lee, Larry French, Tex Carleton, Clay Bryant, and Dizzy Dean came or went during Root's career (1926–1941).

He's best known for throwing Babe Ruth's famous "called shot" home run in Game 3 of the 1932 World Series. Recently uncovered film of the event confirms what most suspected, that Ruth didn't point to center field before he launched his mammoth drive. But Root's name will always be unreasonably judged in one of the most memorable events in baseball history. When they asked Root himself, he provided a definitive answer: "He didn't point. If he had, I'd have knocked him on his fanny. . . . I took my pitching too seriously to have anybody facing me do that."[8]

On August 10, 1941, the Cubs celebrated Root's career. He received a $2,200 check, a blanket, a desk clock, and a pig. Fans bought him a car. When the team released Root at the end of the season he had 201 wins, still the team record. At 42 years old he was the oldest player in the majors and the last born before 1900.

Root played minor-league baseball in 1942. He pitched until his 49th birthday and won 111 games. Later Root coached two short stints with the Cubs. He retired to California and died on November 5, 1970. No Cubs pitcher has caught Root in career wins. And no one probably ever will.

7 Hank O'Day, Phil Cavarretta, and Bob Kennedy managed the Cubs and were born in Chicago. Lou Boudreau (Harvey) and Mike Quade (Evanston) came close.

Phil Cavarretta grew up on Chicago's Near North Side, a short "L" ride from Wrigley Field. He attended Lane Tech High School on Addison Street. Cavarretta led Lane Tech to the 1933 Chicago Public League baseball championship.

During his senior year at Lane in the spring of 1934, Cavarretta tried out for the Cubs at Wrigley Field. The Cubs offered Cavarretta a contract, and to support his family, he quit school for minor-league baseball. He made the big club later that year. In his first start on September 25, Cavarretta smoked a home run to beat the Reds, 1–0. The 18-year-old batted .381 in his short stint with the team.

Cavarretta stayed with the big club for good in 1935. The first baseman joined graybeards like Charlie Root, Gabby Hartnett, and Kiki Cuyler. Cavarretta held his own. He stroked 162 hits and batted .275.

Cavarretta's career fluctuated after that. He lost his starting job in 1937 and missed chunks of 1939 and 1940 with broken ankles. He played full-time again by 1942, both at first base and in the outfield. He batted .355, compiled a .449 onbase percentage, and a 6.0 WAR in 1945. Cavarretta won the National League Most Valuable Player Award and led the Cubs to the World Series. Cavarretta hit .423 in the series, but the Cubs lost to the Tigers in seven games.

Cavarretta continued to excel after World War II. He played in the 1946 and 1947 All-Star Games and hit a combined 7.5 WAR those two years. But then the Cubs collapsed. After four horrible seasons, on July 21, 1951, the Cubs offered the 35-year-old Cavarretta a player-manager position, replacing Frankie Frisch.

Cavarretta fulfilled his greatest baseball moment a week later, on July 29, 1951. He played first base in the first game of a doubleheader against the Phillies and plated three runs in a 5–4 win. In the sixth inning of the nightcap, while Cavarretta coached third, the Cubs loaded the bases. Cavarretta went to the dugout and grabbed a bat. As he strode to the plate to pinch-hit, the fans gave him a massive ovation. Before the cheers died down, Cavarretta drove Robin Roberts's first pitch onto Sheffield Avenue. The Cubs won 8–6 and swept the Phillies.

Cavarretta led the Cubs to a .500 record in 1952, but they lost 89 games the next year. During spring training in 1954, Cavarretta met with P. K. Wrigley. The player-manager told Wrigley the Cubs could not win the pennant. Wrigley called Cavarretta's honesty "defeatist" and immediately removed him as manager. When Cavarretta refused a demotion to manage the team's minor-league Los Angeles team, Wrigley released Cavarretta.

Phil Cavarretta played 20 seasons with the Cubs, the longest in the modern era. He totaled a .292 batting average, 1,927 hits, and a 34 WAR. He still ranks in the Cubs' top 10 in

Phil Cavarretta—the last Cubs player-manager. (National Baseball Hall of Fame, Cooperstown, NY)

games, at-bats, runs, singles, triples, extra base hits, RBIs, and walks. It was a fine career for a true Chicagoan.

8 The supposed Billy Goat curse that kept the Cubs out of the World Series for 71 years had its origins in the 1945 World Series.

Billy Sianis purchased the Lincoln Tavern at 1855 W. Madison Street, across from the old Chicago Stadium. One day a goat tumbled off a truck outside the bar. The story says Sianis's finances changed for the better—the goat brought good luck. Sianis kept the animal and changed the bar's name to the Billy Goat Tavern (Sianis moved his bar to its present Michigan Avenue location in 1964).

Billy Sianis bought his goat a ticket to Game 4 of the 1945 World Series. Sianis got the goat into the ballpark. He draped a blanket over his pet's back that read, "WE GOT DETROIT'S GOAT." As Sianis walked the goat to its seat (tier 12, box 65, seat 6), chief usher Andy Frain threw it out of the park. Sianis left the goat at a nearby parking lot, paid $1 to store him, and went inside to watch the action.

But outside of an off-the-cuff threat to sue the Cubs, no contemporary source mentioned a curse. The entertainment and theater critic of the *Chicago Tribune*, Will Leonard, gave the first reference to a curse on December 26, 1967, 22 years after the incident. Leonard wrote: "But Billy got even by putting a hex on the Cubs. The Cubs lost that World Series and their fortunes plummeted after the war. Finally, Phillip K Wrigley, the owner, asked him to take the hex off. Sianis agreed. It did not seem to help the Cubs until recently."[9]

The longtime sportswriter of the *Chicago Tribune*, David Condon, a friend of Sianis, referenced the restaurateur over

20 times in articles before he mentioned Sianis and a curse in 1969, 15 months after Leonard's story. Condon ingrained the curse in fans' minds when he wrote about it three more times in four years. The goat curse legend mushroomed from there.

The Billy Goat Tavern embraces the curse, which helps attract tourists. That makes it unlikely that Sianis kept quiet about it for over 20 years. It's also improbable that the Chicago media of the 1950s and 1960s wouldn't have latched on to it, especially since it coincided with some of the worst years in Cubs history.

A goat entered and got tossed out of Game 4 of the 1945 World Series. The subsequent story of Billy Sianis's curse, hatched over 20 years after the fact, provides a great yarn, made greater by the Cubs' mediocre play. But logic says it never happened.

9 The Cubs made one of their better trades on June 15, 1949. They sent away two outfielders on the back sides of their careers and obtained two outfielders who delivered 13 combined years of dependable service. Peanuts Lowrey and Harry Walker went to the Reds. Frankie Baumholtz and Hank Sauer came to the Cubs.

The 30-year-old Sauer found himself logjammed in the Reds' minor-league system. He finally joined the team in 1948 and clubbed 66 home runs the next two years. When he started off slow in 1949, the Reds shipped him to the Cubs. The North Siders stationed him in left field and Sauer stroked 27 home runs in a little more than half a season.

Sauer slugged more than 30 home runs each of the next three years, including 37 in 1952. That year he drove in 121 runs with an .892 OPS. Sauer won the National League Most

Valuable Player Award in a close and controversial vote. The three next finishers, Robin Roberts, Joe Black, and Hoyt Wilhelm, all pitchers, split their votes, and Sauer snared a narrow victory.

On June 4, 1953, the Cubs picked up slugger Ralph Kiner in a blockbuster trade with the Pirates. Kiner also hit 37 home runs in 1952, and Cubs fans dreamed of the two big men drilling the buildings across Waveland Avenue. But rather than challenge for pennants in 1953 and 1954, the Cubs lost 89 and 90 games. After the 1954 season, the Cubs sent Kiner to the Indians. A still productive but aging Sauer went to the Cardinals before the 1956 season.

Sauer developed as one of baseball's great late-bloomers. He hit nearly 98 percent of his home runs (281 of 288) after his 30th birthday. No other major leaguer with as many home runs ever came close. Diehard Cubs fans fell for Sauer and his longball power, one of the true joys during really tough years. They called him "The Mayor of Wrigley Field," and bleacher fans showered him with bags of chewing tobacco after each home run.

Sauer died the way we all want to go—stricken by a massive heart attack on a golf course, playing one of the two games he loved.

10 Losing 20 or more games doesn't make you a failure. Hall of Fame pitchers like Walter Johnson, Steve Carlton, Phil Niekro, and Robin Roberts all lost 20 or more games in a season. Of the Cubs pitchers since 1900 who lost that many games, four of them (Tom Hughes, Sam Jones, Dick Ellsworth, and Larry Jackson) won 20 or more games in other years.

Bill Bonham went 11–22 in 1974, the last Cub to lose 20 or more games in a season. It made sense. The 1974 Cubs finished last in the National League East at 66–96 (.407). Rick Reuschel won 13 games. No one else besides Bonham won more than eight. Before the 1974 season, the Cubs "backed up the truck," trading away longtime regulars like Fergie Jenkins, Ron Santo, Glenn Beckert, Randy Hundley, and Jim Hickman. The new baby Cubs averaged just 26 years old, one of the major's youngest teams.

Bonham joined the Cubs in 1971 and spent five years— 1973–1977—in the rotation. Bonham belonged to a quartet of young Cubs pitchers who began their major-league careers from 1971 to 1973. The four—Bonham, Reuschel, Burt Hooton, and Ray Burris—had promise. Jack Brickhouse frequently reminded fans of their "live arms." But live arms wouldn't guarantee success, and each had varying careers with the Cubs and beyond.

Bonham sported a 53–70 record on the Cubs when they traded him to the Reds in 1977. He spent his final three years with a much better Reds team and went 22–13.

Bill Bonham will be the last Cub to lose more than 20 games in a season. The five-man rotation and specialized bullpens limits the games and innings pitchers throw. They don't pitch enough anymore to lose that many games. From 1900 to 1909, 74 major-league pitchers lost at least 20 games. During the 1970s that number dropped to 14. Since 1980 only two pitchers have lost 20 games or more.

Here are the nine Cubs who lost 20 or more games in a season since 1900:

- 1901   Tom Hughes   10–23
- 1917   Phil Douglas   14–20
- 1950   Bob Rush   13–20

- 1955   Sam Jones   14–20
- 1960   Glen Hobbie   16–20
- 1962   Dick Ellsworth   9–20
- 1965   Larry Jackson   14–21
- 1966   Dick Ellsworth   8–22
- 1974   Bill Bonham   11–22

11 This is false. While it's true the Cardinals have won more World Series titles than the Cubs (11 to 3) and more overall championships including those won before the World Series began in 1903 (15 to 9), the Cubs have a better record in head-to-head competition between the two teams. Through the 2016 season, the Cubs lead the all-time regular season series, 1,207–1,156. To put it another way, the Cardinals won more championships, but they didn't necessarily get them by beating the Cubs.

The Cubs and Cardinals go way back. They inaugurated St. Louis's first National League game on April 12, 1892 (the Cubs were the Colts and the Cardinals the Browns). The Colts won the opener 14–10 with outfielder Sam Dungan slapping a single, double, and triple. The Colts swamped the Browns again on August 1, 1894, 26–8. The Chicagoans clubbed 27 hits including seven doubles. Things got so bad for the Browns that infielder Heinie Peitz pitched the final three innings.

The Cubs dominated the Cardinals from 1902 to 1913, winning every season series. The Cubs went 187–69 against the Redbirds during that stretch, one that paralleled both the great Cubs dynasty and one of the Cardinals' worst stretches in history. During those 12 years the Cubs finished above .500 every season except one, while the Cardinals finished below .500 every season except one.

Recent Cubs fans savor the only postseason meeting between the teams, during the 2015 National League Divisional Series. The Cardinals won the Central Division with 100 wins and led the upstart Cubs by three games. After the Cubs rattled the Pirates in the Wild Card Game, they met the Cardinals. The Redbirds won the first game, but the young Cubs scrambled back and won three straight to take the series. It marked a change in direction between the two teams, recently dominated by the Cardinals.

Most Cardinals fans understandably lord their 11 World Series titles over their northern neighbors. But the tide turned in 2015, and when the two teams meet on the field, the Cubs more often than not have come out on top.

12 Why does Wrigley Field survive while every other ballpark from its era besides Fenway Park is long gone? Here are five reasons:

- Cubs owner P. K. Wrigley continually repaired and updated the ballpark. It stayed structurally sound. Other ballparks as old as Wrigley Field, like Connie Mack Stadium in Philadelphia, fell into disrepair or became obsolete. They were too costly to renovate or expand.
- Two attempts to build a modern stadium in Chicago failed. The large multipurpose stadiums built in the 1960s offered modern designs with views unblocked by posts. Thirteen sprang up between 1960 and 1971 (think Riverfront Stadium and Three Rivers Stadium). Mayor Richard J. Daley wanted a multipurpose stadium to house the Cubs, the White Sox, and the Bears, but couldn't get the support of Art Allyn, who owned the

White Sox. Allyn instead wanted to build a privately financed collection of three stadiums. But he couldn't capture Daley's support.

- The new ballparks that replaced the 1960s-era stadiums were an improvement, but still inferior to Wrigley Field. Since 1992, architects have designed these "neo-classic" parks to mimic Wrigley Field: smaller-sized facilities with real grass, bricks, and even manually operated scoreboards. But to accommodate luxury suites, they have upper decks too high and too far from the field. And while they hint at the historical credentials of vintage ballparks (the right field warehouse in Baltimore's Camden Yards), old-time integrity can't be built. Your great-grandparents watched baseball at Wrigley Field. Babe Ruth, Lou Gehrig, and Jackie Robinson played there. That can't be replicated.

- The Cubs would have abandoned Wrigley Field if the surrounding neighborhood had destabilized. But the area gentrified, becoming "Wrigleyville," a trendy place to be and to be seen.

- When the Ricketts family purchased the Cubs in 2009, they promised to rebuild and update Wrigley Field. Ricketts offered to pay for the project as long as he could erect large scoreboards and advertising signage (to cover renovation costs). After a drawn-out battle with the rooftop club owners across the street, the Cubs began renovations in the fall of 2014. The modern updates and expansions allow the 1914-era ballpark to compete with newer ones throughout the majors, and remain the Cubs' home for decades more.

Videoboards brought the 21st century to the Friendly Confines.
(Photo courtesy of Sue Skowronski)

13 On April 21, 1966, the Cubs traded veteran pitchers Bob Buhl and Larry Jackson to the Phillies for first baseman John Herrnstein, fleet-footed outfielder Adolfo Phillips, and hard-throwing Ontario-born Ferguson Jenkins. It's easily one of the five best trades in franchise history.

Jenkins showed promise right out of the gate. In his first game as a Cub on April 23, 1966, he entered in the third inning with the bases loaded. He worked out of the jam and pitched another five shutout innings. Jenkins clubbed a home run and drove in both runs in a 2–0 win.

Later in the season Jenkins cemented a starter's role, winning three games in a 10-game stretch. His 1966 numbers heartened the last-place Cubs: 182 innings and only 147 hits allowed,

148 strikeouts and just 51 walks, and a 1.088 WHIP. The team lost 103 games but Jenkins provided hope for the future.

Jenkins won 20 games in 1967, and duplicated it for the next five years. His ascendancy coincided with the rebirth of the Cubs during the "Cub Power" era. He's most responsible for the Cubs resurgence. For seven years the Cubs roster bulged with future Hall of Famers Ernie Banks, Billy Williams, and Ron Santo. But until Jenkins came along, the Cubs lost far more than they won. Jenkins solidified an inconsistent pitching staff and became the stopper. His presence made the whole team better.

Fergie slipped to 14–16 in 1972, and the Cubs traded him to the Rangers. Jenkins won another 115 major-league games with the Rangers and the Red Sox, and like Mordecai Brown before him, returned to the Cubs to finish up his career. He won 20 games again for the Cubs but needed two years to do it: 1982 and 1983. On May 25, 1982, Jenkins recorded his 3,000th strikeout against Garry Templeton in San Diego. And Jenkins became the first major leaguer to end his career with more than 3,000 strikeouts and fewer than 1,000 walks.

Despite splitting his 19 years between the Cubs and three other teams, Jenkins holds Cubs records for games started (347) and strikeouts (2,038). He's in the team's top 10 in games, innings pitched, victories (167), shutouts, and years of service. Had Jenkins played his entire career on the North Side, he'd own every major Cubs pitching record after the Dead Ball Era.

Jenkins received a plethora of accolades during and after his career. He won the National League Cy Young Award in 1971. He entered the National Baseball Hall of Fame in 1991. The Cubs retired his and Greg Maddux's number 31 uniforms in 2009. In 2011, he appeared on a Canadian postage stamp.

Ferguson Jenkins is easily the greatest Canadian-born major leaguer. And he's the best Cubs pitcher since at least Mordecai "Three Finger" Brown.

14 Don Kessinger collected about 300 at-bats with the 1965 Cubs. The light-hitting shortstop batted just .201, slotted seventh or eighth in the order.

When Kessinger's 1966 season didn't improve much, manager Leo Durocher suggested he try switch-hitting. On May 19 against the Astros, Kessinger grounded weakly to second base and popped out to third batting right-handed. Then he switch-hit, batting left-handed. He flied out to deep center field in the sixth inning and lined out to the shortstop in the eighth. No hits but finally solid outs; a switch-hitter was born. Kessinger hit .299 in August and .346 in September.

Kessinger assumed the leadoff position in August 1966 and stayed there through 1975—10 years. It's the longest stint in Cubs history. Although Kessinger never excelled offensively (.252 average, 14 career home runs, 100 stolen bases), he played consistently with solid defense (Jack Brickhouse marveled at his "boardinghouse reach").

Don's greatest day at the plate occurred at Wrigley Field on June 17, 1971. Kessinger went 6-for-6 in a 7–6 win against the Phillies. Don singled in the first inning, singled in the second, singled in the fourth, singled in the sixth, doubled in the eighth, and singled in the 10th. He scored the game-winning run on a single by Ron Santo. And to reinforce the benefit of switch-hitting, Kessinger stroked his first four hits right-handed, the last two left-handed.

Kessinger collected 1,619 hits as a Cub and won two Gold Glove Awards. As the proto-type defensive shortstop of the

1960s and 1970s, he appeared in six All-Star Games.

The Cubs sent Kessinger to the Cardinals in 1976. The following year he went to the White Sox and served as a player-manager for half the 1979 season (the last player-manager in American League history). He managed the baseball team at the University of Mississippi during the 1990s. In 1992, his son Keith had a stint with the Reds, and he now calls baseball games for Ole Miss.

Don Kessinger—the table-setter for the "Cub Power" teams. (National Baseball Hall of Fame Library, Cooperstown, NY)

Kessinger wasn't the star of the "Cub Power" teams. But he set the table for the big hitters and reached most balls hit his way. The man from Forrest City, Arkansas, was a valuable member of those memorable teams.

15 Eleven brother pairs played on the Cubs (or the White Stockings and Colts), and five of them played at the same time. Here's the list of the brothers and their WAR numbers while they were Cubs:

11. Jiggs Parrott 1892–1895 (–4.1)
    Tom Parrott 1883 (–.4)
10. Danny Breeden 1971 (–.5)
    Hal Breeden 1971 (–.3)
 9. Jim Tyrone 1972, 1974–1975 (–.1)
    Wayne Tyrone 1976 (–.4)

8. Lew Camp 1893–1894 (–.2)
   Kid Camp 1894 (–.2)
7. Jerry Hairston Jr. 2005–2006 (.5)
   Scott Hairston 2013 (–.6)
6. Solly Drake 1956 (.4)
   Sammy Drake 1960–1961 (–.4)
5. Mort Cooper 1949 (0.0)
   Walker Cooper 1954–1955 (2.5)
4. Corey Patterson 2000–2005 (9.6)
   Eric Patterson 2007–2008 (0.0)
3. Ed Sauer 1943–1945 (.1)
   Hank Sauer 1949–1955 (19.3)
2. Larry Corcoran 1880–1885 (28.0)
   Mike Corcoran 1884 (–0.4)
1. Rick Reuschel 1972–1981, 1983–1984 (48.3)
   Paul Reuschel 1975–1978 (1.6)

The winners are the Reuschel brothers from Camp Point, Illinois (49.9 combined WAR). Older brother Paul pitched primarily in relief. He went 12–11 with a 1.438 WHIP and 12 saves. Brother Rick was the workhorse of the Cubs staff for 10 years. Rick went 135–127 with a 1.312 WHIP. He won 20 games in 1977 and 18 more in 1979. Rick is in the Cubs all-time top 10 for games started, innings, hits allowed, walks, and strikeouts.

Rick Reuschel was a big man (easily 230 pounds) but won two Gold Glove Awards after he left the team. He frequently pinch-ran and even pinch-hit on occasions. Both of them took up a lot of space; they easily earned their nicknames "Tall Paul" and "Big Daddy" (although Rick got his famous moniker after he left the Cubs).

Later in this book, I share the most underrated Cubs position players. If I added pitchers, Rick Reuschel would be included. He ranks second all-time in WAR for Cubs pitchers (after Fergie Jenkins) and 10th all-time in Cubs history, right behind Gabby Hartnett and ahead of Mordecai Brown, Frank Chance, and Billy Herman.

Reuschel won 77 games for the Pirates and the Giants from 1985 to 1991. He won 19 games as a 39-year-old, and 17 more the next year. When Reuschel finally called it quits, he was the oldest man in the major leagues at 42 years old. Reuschel compiled a 214–191 record. Had he played his whole career on winning teams, he'd be a marginal Hall of Famer.

16 The Cubs brass of the late-1970s wouldn't recognize an emergent superstar's value if he bit them in the keister. But at least in this instance, the Cubs began with good intentions. After the 1973 season, the Cubs traded away the remnants of their 1969 team. They sent pitcher Fergie Jenkins to the Rangers for two 23-year-old infielders: Vic Harris and Bill Madlock. While they probably traded Jenkins too early in his career, the move would slightly resemble those made by Theo Epstein and Jed Hoyer 40 years later—peddling coveted but older pieces for youngsters with high potential.

Madlock proved to be better than even advertised. The line-drive-hitting third baseman batted a robust .313 in 1974. The next year he won the National League batting title with a .354 average, the highest Cubs batting average in 30 years. Madlock hit .339 in 1976 and won his second consecutive batting title.

Madlock's 1976 title materialized on the season's last day. He trailed the Reds' Ken Griffey Sr. by .005 the morning of

October 3. Griffey sat out that day to preserve the lead, but Madlock singled four times in four at-bats. When Griffey got wind of Madlock's heroics, he came into the game, but struck out twice. Manager Jim Marshall removed Madlock to a standing ovation from the 9,486 fans at Wrigley Field. He won the batting title by .003, .339 to .336.

The free agent era began after the 1976 season, and Madlock looked for an increase in his $80,000 salary. He and his agent (something new in baseball) initially asked for $300,000 a year. The Cubs balked and offered $200,000. Instead of negotiating with Madlock, the Cubs traded him to the Giants for an "old" 30-year-old outfielder, Bobby Murcer. The Cubs paid Murcer $320,000 per year, more than Madlock's initial request. Murcer brought his rocking chair to the Cubs clubhouse and played two passable years in Chicago.

Madlock eventually won two more batting titles with the Pirates, but suffered numerous injuries during a career that traded-off great seasons with disappointing ones. You wonder what would have become of Madlock had the Cubs paid their budding superstar a fair and representative salary. The whole thing smelled of the Greg Maddux debacle in 1992, when a little more negotiating and a little less ego would have locked up the best pitcher in a generation with the Cubs, not the Braves.

Madlock's tied for the highest batting average in Cubs history—.336. His stick would have looked nice in subsequent years, especially in 1984 when the Cubs battled and lost the National League Championship Series to the Padres. Chalk up Madlock as one who got away. At least one the Cubs let get away.

17 Strictly by statistics—OPS—you'd choose Frank Robinson, Willie Mays, Gary Sheffield, or Mark McGwire. All produced OPS numbers over 1.000 against the Cubs during their long careers. But if you went by heads *and* hearts, as in "Who stomped Cubs' hearts year in and year out?"—you'd go with Mike Schmidt.

The Phillies third baseman terrorized the Cubs; his ruinations bring tortuous nightmares to North Siders of a certain age. Schmidt clubbed a .985 OPS against the Cubs and crushed 78 home runs, the most ever against the team. Fifty of his clouts came at Wrigley Field, another record. And it wasn't just numbers. It's the way he did it.

On April 17, 1976, Schmidt slammed four consecutive home runs against the Cubs, the first time it happened in National League history. The Cubs actually led the game after four innings, 13–2. But Schmidt proved that a lead even that big at Wrigley Field wasn't safe with him in the lineup.

Schmidt slammed a two-run home run off Rick Reuschel in the fifth inning. In the seventh he went deep again off Reuschel. His three-run eighth-inning bomb off Mike Garman, into the seldom-reached upper center field bleachers, brought the Phillies to within 13–12. Schmidt's final bit of destruction, a two-run missile off Paul Reuschel (Rick's brother), gave the Phillies a 17–15 lead. The Phillies won, 18–16. Schmidt went 5-for-6 and knocked in eight RBIs.

Schmidt ended his 18-year career with 548 home runs, the most by a third baseman. It's mind-altering to think how many home runs Schmidt would have hit in a Cubs uniform, playing half his games at The Friendly Confines. Between 1977 and 1983 Schmidt hit 27 home runs in just 210 at-bats at Wrigley Field.

One could dream. But then reality creeps in and brings nightmares, haunting images of Schmidt rounding the bases in that horrendous powder blue and red Phillies uniform. Most mature Cubs fans saw far too much of that. In their dreams, and in person, too.

18 The Cubs played baseball's only all-afternoon home schedule from June 15, 1948, to August 8, 1988. Something as seemingly innocuous as the sun affected baseball at Wrigley Field like at no other ballpark. Wrigley Field's orientation, with center field facing northeast, meant bright afternoon games challenged right fielders, who looked directly into the sun. Add fickle winds and most consider Wrigley Field's right field the most difficult position to play in all of baseball.

For years the Cubs and the Chicago media lamented that sunny days sapped the team's energy. Like clockwork the Cubs plummeted in the standings as the season wore on. The Cubs teams of 1969, 1973, 1977, and 1979 saw division leads dwindle as the weather heated up. The 1969 Cubs became kings of collapses, losing 16 games to the Mets in six weeks.

A look at the team's monthly records bears this out. From 1969 to 1979 the Cubs played 10 games over .500 in April, 22 games over .500 in May, and 14 games over .500 in June. But during the second half of the season they played under .500 each month: 17 games under .500 in July, three games under in August, and 44 games under .500 in September, by far their worst month.[10] The Cubs dropped more games as the cumulative effect of day baseball increased.

Statistics from 1989 to 1999, after Wrigley Field added lights, show a less consistent end-of-the-season downturn. The

Cubs worst month was June (−37), the best July (+29). The Cubs lost 13 more games than they won in September: a deficit but one far less than without lights.

Would the 2016 Cubs have won a World Series without lights at Wrigley Field? No one knows for sure. But it wouldn't have been any easier.

19 Some Cubs go together. The power-hitting duos of Billy Williams and Ron Santo, Kris Bryant and Anthony Rizzo; the batteries of Grover Cleveland Alexander and Bill Killefer, Jon Lester and David Ross; and the double play combinations of Ernie Banks and Gene Baker, Don Kessinger and Glenn Beckert. Then there's Bill Buckner and Leon Durham. They're joined by more than just occupying the same dugout. The two share unfortunate twists of fate, and the aftermaths neither deserved.

On January 11, 1977, the Cubs traded Rick Monday and Mike Garman to the Dodgers for Bill Buckner, Ivan DeJesus, and Jeff Albert. Buckner came as damaged goods, his ankles gimpy from two past surgeries. At times he could barely walk, yet he played baseball at its highest level. Buckner won the 1980 National League batting title with a .324 average. In seven years with the Cubs, Buckner clubbed 1,136 hits and averaged .300.

Buckner's best known for his error in Game 6 of the 1986 World Series, playing first base for the Red Sox. It's unfortunate to blemish his fine career (2,715 hits) by that one mistake, especially one that didn't directly lose the series. Red Sox fans and the media brutalized Buckner. The Red Sox finally won a World Series in 2004, and their fans and the press have long since moved on. Now Buckner is a sympathetic character in Boston, as he should be. He even starred in a comical television commercial on the 30-year anniversary of the error. Buckner endured hell. Hopefully now he's at peace.

That brings us to Leon Durham. "The Bull" came to the Cubs in a trade that sent away future Hall of Famer Bruce Sutter. So Durham already had a lot to live up to. And he did. Durham played predominantly in the outfield from 1981 to 1983. He led the Cubs in stolen bases in 1981 and home runs in 1981 and 1982.

Durham replaced Bill Buckner at first base before the 1984 season. That year he drove in 96 runs and slugged an .874 OPS. In the National League Championship Series, the Cubs led the Padres in the seventh inning of Game 5, 3–2. San Diego put a runner on second base with one out. Tim Flannery hit a groundball to Durham at first base. The ball went through his legs. The runner scored and the Padres eventually won the fifth and deciding game, 5–3.

Dugout gossip revealed that Gatorade spilled on Durham's glove earlier in the game, making it sticky and perhaps stiff. That's probably why Durham missed a ball he caught scores and scores of times before. Durham can't be blamed for losing the series to San Diego. He knocked a solo home run in Game 4 and a two-run first-inning clout in Game 5, just two hours earlier.

Buckner and Durham had a lot in common. They both hit left-handed. Both Buckner and Durham started their careers as outfielders and switched to first base. Durham followed Buckner as the Cubs' everyday first baseman. And similar errors in postseason games just two years apart, dogged them for the rest of their careers and beyond. Buckner has moved past the incident. Now that the Cubs have won their elusive World Series, Durham should too.

20 Adding lights at Wrigley Field allowed the Cubs to host the 61st Major League All-Star Game on July 10, 1990. The Cubs and the city expected a windfall of $35 million from the event.

The All-Star Game provided little drama. The National League broke a dubious All-Star Game record with just two hits. The only extra base hit—a double by Julio Franco—drove in both runs in a 2–0 American League victory. Add a one-hour rain delay and the game bored just about everyone (if only the wind had blown out).

Many fans without All-Star Game tickets purchased seats to "Workout Day," the Monday afternoon event before Tuesday night's game. Those fans watched batting practice, an Old-Timers' game, and the home-run-hitting contest. The latter included the American League's Ken Griffey Jr., Cecil Fielder, Jose Canseco, and Mark McGwire against the National League's Matt Williams, Bobby Bonilla, Darryl Strawberry, and Ryne Sandberg.

This early version of the home-run contest wasn't the event it is today: it didn't sell out, it took place in the afternoon, and each batter got just five outs. The eight All-Stars smacked five home runs. McGwire and Williams each hit one. Sandberg won the contest with three. After making two outs, he poked one into the left field bleachers and then crushed two onto Waveland Avenue.

Ryne Sandberg provided a career full of excitement for Cubs fans. Sandberg stroked a .285 average, 2,385 hits, 282 home runs, a .795 OPS, and 67.7 WAR. A do-it-all second baseman, Sandberg both broke defensive records and led the 1990 National League with 40 home runs. He played in ten consecutive All-Star Games and won nine consecutive Gold Gloves. Sandberg entered the National Baseball Hall of Fame in 2005.

Sandberg dreamed of the chance to manage the Cubs. And to realize it he did what few Hall of Famers ever attempted—to learn managing from the bottom up. In 2007 Sandberg managed the Cubs' Single-A team in Peoria, in 2009 at Double-A Tennessee, and in 2010 at Triple-A Iowa. When the Cubs filled their top position in 2011, Sandberg thought the job was his to lose. The Cubs went another direction and hired interim manager Mike Quade.

Sandberg moved to the Phillies organization and managed their major-league club from August 16, 2013 to June 26, 2015. He fulfilled his dream, just not on the North Side. When the Phillies fired Sandberg, he moved back into the Cubs organization, where he really always belonged.

21 Opening Day is the best day of the year. Fans wonder "Who's new?", "Who's improved?", and "What are our chances?" Hope fills the air.

The most exhilarating Opening Day breakout in team history occurred on April 4, 1994. That day a little-known outfielder penciled his name into the record books. Karl "Tuffy" Rhodes brought Wrigley Field fans to their feet with a first-inning homer off Cubs nemesis Dwight Gooden. Rhodes raked another bomb in the third inning. He drove the crowd into convulsions with a fifth-inning blast off Gooden. His surreal three-peat stopped play as the grounds crew scooped up

Karl "Tuffy" Rhodes— greatest power-laden opener in baseball history. (National Baseball Hall of Fame Library, Cooperstown, NY)

hats, trash, and give-away magnetic schedules that littered the outfield. Rhodes had slugged home runs his first three at-bats of the season, a feat never done before or since in major-league history

The Cubs lost to the Mets that Opening Day, 12–8. And fans who asked "Who's improved" on Opening Day weren't answering "Tuffy Rhodes" in June. Rhodes's fortunes dried up and Glenallen Hill replaced him before the first day of summer. Tuffy played just intermittently after that and the Cubs waived him on May 26, 1995. The Red Sox picked up Rhodes, but waived him soon after. Rhodes's career seemed over with just 13 home runs including those three knocks on that magical Opening Day.

But Rhodes got one more chance. He signed with the Kintetsu Buffalo of the Nippon Professional League. Either Japanese baseball officials knew something their American counterparts did not, or they got extremely lucky. Rhodes went crazy in Japan, and played the next 13 years like he did at that Wrigley Field opener. He hit 464 home runs, the most ever by a foreign player. Rhodes even tied the great Sadaharu Oh's one-season 55-home-run mark in 2001.

There's a lesson here. If someone hits three home runs on Opening Day, they're probably pretty good. Or maybe the Japanese leagues are inferior to their North American counterparts. In either case, Tuffy Rhodes put on a show. And odds are that Rhodes's 1994 Opening Day home-run binge will never be duplicated, in the United States or in Japan.

22 It's a fact that Cubs fans loved him. But he'll be forgotten decades from now by everyone except a handful of old-timers, just like Bill Nicholson and Andy Pafko today. Overshadowed by Ryne Sandberg, Andre Dawson, and Sammy Sosa when he played, he made his mark with boyish looks, consistent play, and his pride in wearing a Cubs uniform.

The Cubs took Mark Grace in the 24th round of the 1985 draft. A real longshot, he debuted on May 2, 1988, and wrestled the first baseman's job from Leon Durham. Grace stroked 144 hits his first season and finished second to Chris Sabo in the National League Rookie of the Year balloting.

Grace batted .314 (.862 OPS) and helped the Cubs win the 1989 National League East title. In the five-game playoff loss to the Giants, he went 11-for-17, batted .647, and stroked a phenomenal 1.799 OPS. After that remarkable performance he more than earned the nickname, "Amazing Grace."

Criticized unfairly for not matching the power of teammates Sandberg, Dawson, and Sosa, Grace instead hit line drives. He holds the record for most hits, doubles, and sacrifice hits in the 1990s. The roll call of players who led a decade in hits includes members of baseball's nobility: Honus Wagner, Ty Cobb, Rogers Hornsby, Paul Waner, Lou Boudreau, Richie Ashburn, Roberto Clemente, Pete Rose, Robin Yount, Mark Grace, and Ichiro Suzuki. It's a remarkable group; all of them Hall of Fame worthy except Grace.

Grace twice filed for free agency. Each time Cubs management balked at giving him "superstar money" like his power-laden teammates, but they eventually signed him. Grace's popularity gave them little choice. But Grace and the Cubs parted ways after the 2000 season—he desperately wanted to play for a winner. Grace signed with the Diamondbacks and helped them claim the 2001 World Series. Two years later he retired and became a Diamondbacks' television color man. He worked nine seasons until a drinking problem sidetracked his post-playing career.

Mark Grace built a commendable 13-year record with the Cubs. He was consistent: a .308 average, 2,201 hits, 148 home runs, and a .832 OPS. He was elegant: four Gold Glove Awards at first base. He was loyal: He loved to be a Chicago Cub when at times, Cubdom festered frustration. Most Cubs fans felt bittersweet when the Diamondbacks won their World Series title. Grace finally got his ring, but they wished it had happened while he was in blue pinstripes.

23 This isn't subjective. There's only one answer.

Since Harry Caray's death in 1998, the Cubs have invited celebrities to sing "Take Me Out to the Ballgame." The singers and their voices ran the gamut. Some performed wonderfully, like Vin Scully and Eddie Vedder. Others performed outstandingly bad. Here are the three worst.

- On July 5, 1998, former Chicago Bears head coach Mike Ditka sang the song like he was speed ~~reading singing~~ yelling. Ditka got to the television booth at the last second and rushed the song. For some reason he yelled it like a drill sergeant on uppers.

- Only one singer got thoroughly booed. That was NAS-CAR's Jeff Gordon on May 24, 2005. Gordon started off on the wrong foot when he incorrectly introduced the song: "Hello Chicago! It's great to be here at Wrigley Stadium." Then he sang a version flatter than a blown out Goodyear tire.

- But the absolute worst belonged to singer Ozzy Osbourne. On September 17, 2003, Osbourne (and wife Sharon) sang a version that hardly resembled the original song.

Either Ozzy forgot the words, he never knew them, or his brain wavered into some far-off, desolate universe. Here's his half-decipherable version:

"All right Chicago! Let's . . . I want to hear a real crazy crowd start singing with me. . . . Are you ready? Are you ready? I can't hear you. Are you ready? 2, 3 . . . Let's go out to the ballgame. Let's go out to the crowd . . . Take . . . (Grunting . . .) I don't care . . . (Much more grunting) . . . for its real, 2, 3 strikes you out at the old Ballgame. Aaa! . . . Yea, let's get some runs. Don't mess around, let's get some runs guys."[11]

24 Here are some depressing facts. The 2012 Cubs lost 101 games, one of only three Cubs teams to drop more than 100 since 1876. The 2011–2013 teams earned the third worst three-year record in team history (198–288). The 2010–2014 Cubs finished last every year.

So it's understandable that on April 23, 2014, only 32,323 fans showed up on such an important day—the 100th anniversary of Wrigley Field's first game.

The diehards who attended imbibed in a memorable afternoon. A huge banner draped above the marquee spelled out the centennial slogan, "It's the Party of the Century." A 400-pound cake in the likeness of Wrigley Field stood at the Clark and Addison entrance. Fans sang "Happy Birthday" to the ballpark during the seventh-inning stretch. Everyone received a celebratory cupcake and a replica 1914 Chicago Federal League jersey.

One hundred years earlier the Chicago Federals had thumped the Kansas City Packers, 9–1. One hundred years later, the Diamondbacks turned two singles, a triple, two walks, and an error into five ninth-inning runs and beat the Cubs, 7–5. Trevor Cahill pitched scoreless seventh and eighth innings for the win. The following season Cahill and catcher Miguel Montero played for the Cubs.

The Cubs that day didn't look anything like the team that tore through the National League in 2015 and 2016. Instead of Manager Joe Maddon, Rick Renteria led the squad. Mike Olt patrolled third base, and Darwin Barney held down second. The outfield consisted of Junior Lake, Emilio Bonifacio, and Justin Riggiano.

Wrigley Field wasn't the same ballpark either. The Cubs were still fighting with the rooftop owners across Waveland and Sheffield Avenues. There was no giant video board above the left field bleachers, no plaza, and no renovated bleachers. The Cubs clubhouse was archaic and undersized.

The Wrigley Field centennial celebration already seems decades old. The changes to the team and to the ballpark stagger the imagination. The world champion Cubs now play in a packed Wrigley Field, renovated and ready for another century of action.

3

TRIPLES LEVEL

(Answers begin on page 95.)

Here's where we separate the men from the boys and the women from the girls. You had to have been paying attention or done some digging to know these. Educated guesses might still work, but if you came aboard the Cubs Express in 2016, you're in over your head. The bullpen is warming up, just in case.

1. Who led the Cubs in RBIs for 14 straight seasons?
2. What Cubs had these nicknames: Piano Legs and Reindeer?
3. When did they erect the famous Wrigley Field marquee?
4. When did organ music first play at Wrigley Field?
5. The Cubs went 21–1 against the _____ to secure the 1945 National League pennant?
6. Why did the Cubs lose Game 7 of the 1945 World Series?
7. When was the first Cubs game televised?
8. What was the largest single-game paid attendance in Wrigley Field history?
9. What Cubs had these nicknames: Peanuts and Bear Tracks?
10. Name the first African Americans to play for the Cubs.
11. What Cub became the first African American to pitch a major-league no-hitter?
12. What Cub struck out six times in one game?
13. Who spent the most days inside Wrigley Field?
14. Who was the first Latin player on the Cubs?
15. When did two Latin players lead the Cubs in RBIs? When did three Latin players?
16. What Cubs pitcher led the team in wins during the 1960s?
17. Who was the oldest man to play for the Cubs?
18. When did Murphy's Bleachers open?
19. What's unique about Doug Dascenzo?

20. Despite the fact the Cubs lost 101 games in 2012, what relief pitcher went 7–1 that year?

21. How many years did the Cubs go between being no-hit?

22. Who is the Cubs all-time pinch-hit leader?

23. Who hit the longest home run out of Wrigley Field?

24. Name the most underrated Cub of all time.

TRIPLES LEVEL ANSWERS

1 It's impossible to hyperbolize Cap Anson. Born in a log cabin in Marshalltown, Iowa, in 1852, he played first base and served as player-manager for the Chicago National League team for more than 19 years. Anson's the most prominent and controversial 19th-century baseball figure, and the greatest Cub before Ernie Banks.

Adrian Anson played third base with the Rockford Forest Citys team in 1871, in the inaugural year of the National Association (a forerunner to the National League). He moved to the Philadelphia Athletics and then came to Chicago in 1876, recruited by manager Albert Spaulding to play for the White Stockings in the first year of the National League.

Anson adroitly managed the White Stockings beginning in 1879. His teams won National League pennants in 1880, 1881, 1882, 1885, and 1886. Anson held high expectations of his players in an age when baseball attracted roughhewed characters. He led by example, and others followed and respected him. His colleagues called him "Cap" (short for "captain").

When he retired in 1897, Anson's had set many benchmarks for others to chase. Including his National Association games, he played a record 27 straight years of de facto major-league baseball. Anson became the first major leaguer to stroke 3,000 hits, the first to win four batting titles, and he held the league record for games played, hits, doubles, runs, and RBIs. He still holds the Chicago franchise records for runs scored, hits, singles, doubles, and RBIs. Anson led the Chicago Nationals in RBIs for 14 consecutive years (1880–1893).

Cap's persuasive influence over the franchise led to some of its early nicknames. When Anson joined the team in 1876, fans called them the White Stockings. When Anson obtained younger players in 1890, sportswriters and fans generally called them the "Colts." After the popular Anson departed the franchise in 1897, sportswriters referred to them as the "Orphans."

Anson's extensive power, however, helped restrict black players in organized baseball. On two occasions in the 1880s, Anson protested the presence of black players in exhibition games. At least one black player left a game that Anson protested, and dark-skinned players disappeared from the professional game until 1947. Anson strongly influenced that unwritten practice.

Cap Anson was the towering figure in early baseball, and had an enormous influence, both good and bad, on the game and on the Chicago franchise. He had been dead for 17 years when he entered the National Baseball Hall of Fame in 1939 with his mentor, Albert Spaulding.

2 George Gore had the moxie to negotiate a contract to play for the White Stockings during an exhibition game against the team. White Stockings' president Albert

Adrian "Cap" Anson—the original "Mr. Cub." (National Baseball Hall of Fame Library, Cooperstown, NY)

Spaulding offered $1,200. Gore asked for $2,500. They compromised at $1,900. With it, Gore became one of the first holdouts in major-league history.

Gore played center field for the White Stockings from 1879 to 1886. He led the National League in hitting, on-base percentage, and slugging percentage in 1880. Gore topped the league in runs scored in 1881 and 1882, and walks in 1882, 1884, and 1886. He excelled in many facets of the game, and used his physique, especially his large powerful legs, to propel his game. George "Piano Legs" Gore became the first of only two major leaguers to steal seven bases in a game, and the first to slug five extra base hits.

But Gore also had weaknesses. He committed 368 errors, the most ever by a major-league outfielder (he gets a pass considering the substandard playing fields and equipment of the day). The freewheeling Gore also drank, caroused, and generally got under manager Anson's skin. Anson finally had enough and shipped Gore to the New York Giants.

The Cubs traded for Bill Killefer on December 11, 1917. He came from the Phillies with the legendary pitcher Grover Cleveland Alexander, the prized participant in the trade. They arrived as a package deal, since Killefer acted as Alexander's personal catcher (not unlike the role David Ross played for Jon Lester in 2016). The nine-year veteran

Bill Killefer. (Photo Courtesy of the Library of Congress)

played solid defense and had some speed for a catcher. The latter explains "Reindeer Bill."

Killefer replaced Johnny Evers as Cubs manager on August 4, 1921. He piloted the Cubs nearly four years and compiled a 300–293 record. That's the 16th-best winning percentage (.506) of 54 managers in Cubs history. But Killefer quit during the 1925 season as the Cubs spiraled toward last place. Later Killefer managed the St. Louis Browns. After that he managed and coached in the minors, and became a scout.

3 Only Yankee Stadium's Monument Park and Fenway's Green Monster equal Wrigley Field's ivy for *interior* ballpark acclaim. And nothing on the *exterior* of any major-league stadium before or since equals Wrigley Field's marquee. It endures as one of the most iconic symbols in all of Major League Baseball. Hung in 1934 and originally painted a green-blue color, it stands sentinel at the corner of Clark and Addison Streets, greeting fans or passersby to the oldest ballpark in the National League.

The bottom half of the marquee had interchangeable panels. Early on the panel that read "Chicago Cubs," as in, "Wrigley Field Home of Chicago Cubs" changed during the fall to "Chicago Bears" ("Wrigley Field Home of Chicago Bears"). Throughout the baseball and football seasons the lower panels displayed a sales pitch ("Tickets Now All Games"), the next team the Cubs or Bears played, and the dates of the games. During winter, the lower panel displayed generic messages: "Seasons Greetings," "Prevent Fires," "Drive Safely," or "US Savings Bonds Now for Your Future."

The marquee modernized beginning in 1983. An electronic message board replaced the two lower panels. Beer ads hung below the message board for a few years, the marquee's first non-baseball advertisements. Workers refurbished the marquee again before the 2016 season. They removed it, repainted it, rewired it, and added an LED message board. On the back side that's visible to the seating bowl, they painted a replica in its original green-blue color.

The marquee's color changed over the years. It became dark blue in 1938. It became red in 1965. They painted it purple temporarily for the 2010 Northwestern-Illinois football game. They painted it to its original green-blue color for a few days near the park's 100th anniversary celebration.

The Wrigley Field marquee stands as a lovable symbol of the ballpark. Before and after games, fans flock to the corner of Clark and Addison to photograph this evolving relic. Even on non-game days, it's common to see a taxi pull up in front of the ballpark, a fan get out, take a photograph of the marquee, and quickly reenter the cab before it drives away. That's pretty cool!

4 In one of P. K. Wrigley's innovations to make Wrigley Field a fun and friendly destination, the Cubs brought the first organ to a major-league ballpark. On April 26, 1941, Ray Nelson played an organ behind the screen in back of home plate. He finished his mini-concert 30 minutes before the start of the game so radio broadcasts didn't pick up the ASCAP-copyrighted songs.

Nelson played again the following day; then the team went on a road trip. Nelson planned to play non-copyrighted songs the next homestand, so he could entertain throughout the game. But after the road trip, the organ had disappeared. The Cubs ditched the keyboard after only two days, so not to cross the musicians' union.

Organ music returned in 1967. Jack Kearney played the keyboard located in the old football press box along the third base line. That year also marked the first year outside of World War II that the team played the National Anthem before each home game. They've played it ever since.

Gary Pressy plays the Wrigley Field organ today, and has for 30 years. Fans heard far less of Pressy the last two seasons, because the new video board and the players' walk-up songs play during the traditional "dead" times between batters and between innings. But by offering organ music well into the 21st century, the Cubs are still in the minority.

Here's a list of Wrigley Field organists:

- Ray Nelson   1941
- Jack Kearney   1967–1969
- Frank Pellico*   1970–1975
- Vance Fothergill   1976–1978
- John Henzl   1979–1981
- Ed Vodicka   1982–1983
- Bruce Miles   1984–1986
- Gary Pressy**   1987–date

*   Frank Pellico has played the organ at Chicago Blackhawks hockey games since 1991.

**   Gary Pressy hasn't missed a Cubs game in his 30-year career.

5 How did the Cubs win the 1945 National League pennant? Here are four reasons:

- The 1945 Cubs lost no All-Star-caliber players to World War II, while the three-time National League champion Cardinals endured the whole 1945 season without Stan

Musial, Enos Slaughter, and Terry Moore. The Cubs went just 6–16 against the Cardinals, yet held them off by three games.

- Pitcher Hank Borowy came from the Yankees on July 27 and led the charge down the stretch. Borowy went 56–30 in three-plus years in New York, but the Yankees traded him to the Cubs because he stopped pitching complete games. Borowy went 11–2 for the Cubs (and threw 11 complete games). He won seven games in September, including a 3–0 record against the Cardinals.
- The lowly Reds vaulted the Cubs to the 1945 National League pennant. The Cubs played the Reds 22 times and went 21–1. The Cubs played seven doubleheaders against the Reds and went 14–0. If the teams had gone 11–11 against each other, the Cubs would have finished the season 88–66, seven games behind the Cardinals.
- The Cubs gained momentum as the season wore on. They were 26–6 in July, including winning streaks of 11, six, and five games. The Cubs led the Cardinals by three games on September 1. They went 22–10 in September and maintained their three-game lead. The Cubs finished 98–56 (.636), their best winning percentage from 1936 to 2015. They earned a World Series date with the Tigers.

6 The 1945 Cubs should have won the World Series. The Cubs won 96 games during the regular season. The Detroit Tigers won just 88. The Cubs best 10 players led the best 10 Tigers in WAR, 41.5 to 34.7. And due to wartime travel restrictions the Cubs got a real advantage—they played the last four games of the series at Wrigley Field.

The Cubs held a big advantage in starting pitching. They had four pitchers with a total WAR over 3.5: Claude Passeau (5.0), Hank Wyse (5.0), Ray Prim (3.8), and Hank Borowy (3.8). Borowy entered the series as the team's hottest pitcher, and the Cubs relied on him down the stretch. The Tigers had only one pitcher with a 3.5 or better WAR. But Hal Newhouser sported an out-of-this-world 12.0 total WAR and won his second-consecutive American League Most Valuable Player Award. The Cubs knew the Tigers would rely on Newhouser to carry the pitching load during the series.

In Game 1 in Detroit, Borowy picked up where he left off in the regular season. He threw a six-hit shutout and surprisingly trounced Newhouser, 9–0. After Hank Wyse lost Game 2, 4–1, Claude Passeau pitched the best game to that date in postseason history, a one-hitter that subdued the Tigers, 3–0.

The Cubs came home ahead two games to one, and played every subsequent game at Wrigley Field. But the Tigers conquered Ray Prim in Game 4, 4–1. Borowy's magic ran out in Game 5 as Newhouser leveled him, 8–4. The Cubs had to win Game 6 and they did, 8–7. But it cost the Cubs pitching staff. All four starters—Passeau, Wyse, Prim, and Borowy—pitched. Borowy threw four shutout innings in relief for the win.

In the Game 7 finale, manager Charlie Grimm once again went to his "hot" pitcher, Hank Borowy. It was a major mistake. Blistered and fatigued, Borowy didn't record an out. Newhouser and the Tigers routed the Cubs 9–3 to win the series, four games to three.

Charlie Grimm should have started 22-game winner Hank Wyse in Game 7 instead of the battle-scarred Borowy. Wyse pitched only six innings in Game 2 and only 2/3 of an inning in Game 6. Borowy pitched 18 innings in three games, including nine innings in the last two games. Hindsight admittedly produces a clearer vision, but Wyse was a better choice and a better-rested choice.

A tired Newhouser pitched just well enough in Game 7. Wyse could have won. But due to Grimm's insistence on sticking with his "hot" pitcher, we'll never know.

7 Television was in its infancy in 1939 when two primitive stations started in Chicago. Station W9XBK had no schedule and no programming, but served as a training ground for experimentation with the new medium. The station even gave up its facilities during World War II, but it hardly mattered to Chicagoans. Only 12 televisions existed in the whole city in 1943.

After the war, W9XBK opened as the city's first commercial station, WBKB. The emergent station needed programs. Chicago Cubs owner P. K. Wrigley supported television and saw baseball's potential in it. He offered WBKB free rights to broadcast Cubs games for two years in exchange for the station's continued development of televised baseball.

On April 20, 1946, WBKB tried to televise the Cubs' home opener, but interference from an elevator in the studio's downtown office kept them from broadcasting a clear signal.

WBKB televised its first game on July 13. During a 4–3 loss to the Dodgers, a single camera in Wrigley Field's upper deck focused on home plate, the pitcher's mound, and the right side of the field. The television viewer missed much of the action, and commentator Jack Gibney described what the camera didn't. During the second inning, the station tried a more powerful camera. But it forced the cameraman to shift back and forth between the pitcher and the batter. WBKB went back to the original camera in the third inning.

While many major-league teams limited or blocked televised baseball games, believing it harmed attendance, P. K. Wrigley knew better. He welcomed television and likened it to free advertising. WBKB televised every Cubs home game in 1947, with "Whispering" Joe Wilson and Jack Brickhouse at the microphones. Brickhouse moved to fledgling station WGN when it televised Cubs home games in 1948. A third television station, WENR, televised Cubs home games in 1949. Joe Wilson continued at WBKB, Brickhouse at WGN, and ex-Cub Rogers Hornsby at WENR. Brickhouse and WGN gained the exclusive rights to televise Cubs games by 1952. Brickhouse held that coveted job until 1981.

More than 40 million fans watched the FOX Sports feed of Game 7 of the 2016 World Series. The network used 75 microphones and dozens of cameras, of which nine had super-slow-motion speeds. Baseball and television have come a long way. And it all started from very humble beginnings.

8 On June 27, 1930, 51,556 shoehorned into Wrigley Field to see the Cubs battle the Dodgers. But only 19,748 paid to get in. It was Ladies Day, a regular Friday event that let women in free. The glut of female fans around the park blocked paying customers from the ticket offices. And once fans got there, no tickets remained. "Free" meant something during the Depression, and women flocked to Wrigley Field on Ladies Day to see the winning Cubs.

The largest *paid* single game crowd—47,101—witnessed one of the most significant events in Wrigley Field history—Jackie Robinson's first game in Chicago. Robinson came up with the Dodgers that season, and as the first African-American player in the 20th century, drew large and enthusiastic crowds.

His May 18, 1947, appearance filled the ballpark. Many black fans visited Wrigley Field for the first time, and swelled the crowd.

The Cubs had planned for this day for quite a while. Though they had played games at Comiskey Park, Negro League teams did not play at Wrigley Field until 1942 and 1943. Greats like Satchel Paige, Josh Gibson, and Lester Lockett finally had the chance to showcase their talents on the North Side. These early games were a trial run for the ballpark, the neighborhood, and the fans. Would black fans come north to Wrigley Field for a National League game? How would the neighborhood and North Side fans treat African Americans in their ballpark?

A month before Robinson's first appearance, Fay Young of the *Chicago Defender*, the city's largest African-American newspaper, cautioned that black fans attending Robinson's first game would be scrutinized as much as Jackie. Young understood the significance the ballgame carried. He wrote: "The Negro fan can help Robinson. The Negro fan can ruin him. Robinson is an American citizen, an ex-army officer, a ball player and a gentleman. Let us try and meet his qualifications as a gentleman. If you Chicagoans have got to raise a lot of hell, do a lot of cussing, go somewhere else."[12]

While Robinson played poorly (0-for-4 hitting, an error at first base), the fans came through. Security didn't report a single racial issue in the stands, and the Cubs called it the best-natured large crowd in team history. The fans also scored for the concessions department. That day hungry customers of all stripes purchased 48,000 hot dogs, 72,000 bottles of pop, 17,000 bottles of beer, 13,000 bags of peanuts, and 7,000 bags of popcorn.

9 Native Californian Harry Lowrey joined the Cubs in 1942. The small-in-stature outfielder (named "Peanuts") entered the Army after the 1943 season but returned to the Cubs in 1945 to share outfield duties with Andy Pafko and Bill Nicholson. Lowry drove in 89 runs and helped vault the Cubs to the pennant. He batted .310 in the 1945 World Series.

Lowrey collected 722 hits and a .705 OPS with the Cubs. He played in Chicago until 1949, when the Cubs traded him to the Reds with Harry Walker for Frank Baumholtz and Hank Sauer. After he retired in 1955, he became a base coach for the Phillies, Giants, and Expos. A later generation of Cubs fans knew him when he returned in 1970 to coach at Wrigley Field. Lowrey logged three stints as a Cubs base coach until a heart attack forced him to retire for good in 1981. He died of heart failure in 1986, weeks after open heart surgery.

Lowrey's offseason Southern California home gave him the opportunity to appear in various baseball movies as an extra, a double, or a stuntman. Lowery earned bit parts in five movies, including *Pride of the Yankees*, *The Jackie Robinson Story*, and *The Winning Team*, a biopic about ex-Cub Grover Cleveland Alexander.[13]

Johnny Schmitz had two memorable characteristics: his tight-breaking curveball and his size 14 shoes. His substantial feet and his youth spent in Northern Wisconsin gave him the nickname "Bear Tracks."

The trim left-hander arrived in Chicago just before World War II and stayed a decade. He lost three years to the war but pitched competitively on the Cubs. Schmitz lost 18 games in 1947, but won 18 the following year. In that high watermark 1948 season, he threw 18 complete games and beat the 1949 National League champion Dodgers six times.

Schmitz persevered on some very poor Cubs teams. In the years he played, the Cubs achieved only one winning season. Schmitz ended up like Dick Ellsworth and Rick Reuschel after him, a good pitcher who would have won more if he played on better teams. The Cubs traded Schmitz to the Dodgers in 1951. But by then Schmitz's skills had diminished and he bounced around from the Dodgers, to the Yankees, Reds, Senators, Red Sox, and Orioles. He finished his Cubs career with a 69–80 record, 93–114 overall.

Here are more nicknames of current Cubs and those who played five or more years with the team.

Adrian Anson "Cap"	1876–1897
Frank Flint "Silver"	1879–1892
Mike Kelly "King"	1882–1886
Frank Chance "The Peerless Leader"	1898–1912
Johnny Evers "The Crab"	1902–1913
Mordecai Brown "Three Finger"	1904–1912, 1916
Frank Schulte "Wildfire"	1904–1916
Jim Vaughn "Hippo"	1913–1921
Grover Cleveland Alexander "Pete"	1918–1926
Earl Adams "Sparky"	1922–1927
Leo Hartnett "Gabby"	1922–1940
Guy Bush "The Mississippi Mudcat"	1923–1934
Charlie Grimm "Jolly Cholly"	1925–1936
Lewis Wilson "Hack"	1926–1931
Riggs Stephenson "Old Hoss"	1926–1934
Hazen Cuyler "Kiki"	1928–1935
Lon Warneke "The Arkansas Hummingbird"	1930–1936, 1942–1943, 1945
Stan Hack "Smiling Stan"	1932–1947

Bill Lee "Big Bill"	1934–1943
Phil Cavarretta "Philabuck"	1934–1953
Bill Nicholson "Swish" or "Big Bill"	1939–1948
Dom Dallessandro "Dim Dom"	1940–1944, 1946–1947
Andy Pafko "Handy Andy" or "Pruschka"	1943–1951
Hank Sauer "The Mayor of Wrigley Field"	1949–1955
Ransom Jackson "Handsome Ransom"	1950–1955, 1959
Omar Lown "Turk"	1951–1954, 1956–1958
Don Elston "Every Day"	1953, 1957–1964
Gene Baker "Bango"	1953–1957
Ernie Banks "Mr. Cub" or "Bingo"	1953–1971
Walt Moryn "Moose"	1956–1960
Billy Williams "Sweet Swingin'"	1959–1974
Glenn Beckert "Bruno"	1965–1973
Randy Hundley "Rebel"	1966–1973, 1976–1977
Phil Regan "The Vulture"	1968–1972
Jim Hickman "Gentleman Jim"	1968–1973
Bill Buckner "Billy Buck"	1977–1984
Leon Durham "Bull"	1981–1988
Keith Moreland "Zonk"	1982–1987
Ryne Sandberg "Ryno" or "Kid Natural"	1982–1994, 1996–1997
Steve Trout "Rainbow"	1983–1987
Gary Matthews "The Sarge"	1984–1988
Rick Sutcliffe "The Red Baron"	1984–1991
Andre Dawson "Hawk"	1987–1992
Mark Grace "Amazing" or "Gracie"	1988–2000
Carlos Zambrano "Big Z"	2001–2011
Derrek Lee "D Lee"	2004–2010
Jeff Samardzija "Shark"	2008–2014
Kyle Hendricks "The Professor"	2014–present
Kris Bryant "Sparkles"	2015–present
Kyle Schwarber "Warbird" or "Schwarbs"	2015–present

Kris "Sparkles" Bryant. (Photo courtesy of Sue Skowronski)

10 The success of Jackie Robinson's first appearance at Wrigley Field on May 18, 1947, didn't nudge the Cubs to integrate their team. No clubs besides the Dodgers desegregated quickly (only the Indians and the Browns added a black player in 1947 or 1948). Late in 1947, the Cubs gave a tryout to John Ritchey, a catcher with the Chicago American League Giants of the Negro Leagues. But the team didn't sign him, and Ritchey settled for being the first black player to play in the Pacific Coast League.

Three more years passed before the slow-moving Cubs signed a black player (infielder Gene Baker) and six years before an African American played for the Cubs (the Cubs were the eighth of 16 teams to have at least one black player on their roster). On September 17, 1953, Ernie Banks played shortstop for the Cubs. Gene Baker waited three more days due to an injury.

Gene Baker won the Cubs' second base job and showed consistency, sure hands, and a steady bat. Banks and Baker teamed as an excellent double play combination (called "Bingo and Bango" by radioman Bert Wilson). Baker even earned a spot in the 1955 All-Star Game. On May 1, 1957, the Cubs traded the nearly 32-year-old Baker with Dee Fondy to the Pirates for Dale Long and Lee Walls.

Ernie Banks provided an immediate and long-lasting impact. He slugged 44 home runs in 1955 and shattered the image of the slap-hitting shortstop 30 years before Cal Ripken. Banks went on to become Mr. Cub, the most revered player in team history.

The following black players saw action with the Cubs in the 1950s. All were African-American except Tony Taylor, a native Cuban.

- Ernie Banks   1953–1971
- Gene Baker   1953–1957
- Sam Jones   1955–1956
- Solly Drake   1956
- Monte Irvin   1956
- Lou Jackson   1958–1959
- Tony Taylor   1958–1960
- George Altman   1959–1962, 1965–1967
- Don Eaddy   1959
- Billy Williams   1959–1974

Banks's, Jones's, and Baker's WAR numbers finished one, three, and four on the 1955 Cubs. Because of their success, the "floodgates" for blacks, as it were, opened in 1956 when outfielders

Solly Drake and veteran Monte Irvin joined the Cubs. During the home opener against the Reds on April 20, 1956, the Cubs fielded a majority African-American lineup for the first time. Banks, Baker, Jones, Drake, and Irvin started that afternoon. Both Banks and Irvin cracked home runs, and Jones pitched a complete game, 12–1 win.

11 Chicago Cubs pitchers tossed 15 no-hitters through 2016. Sam "Toothpick" Jones threw the craziest one, against the Pirates on May 12, 1955. Jones became the first African American to throw a major-league no-hitter.

Jones traveled a unique path to the Wrigley Field mound that day. He did not play organized baseball until he served on a Florida Army base during World War II. After his military obligation, Jones pitched two years for the Cleveland Buckeyes of the Negro American League. He joined a traveling Negro League team in 1949 and even pitched in Panama during the offseason. Later that year, Jones tried out for the Cleveland Indians. They signed him and he hurled in minor-league towns like Wilkes-Barre, San Diego, and Indianapolis.

Jones finished the 1951 season with the Indians but pitched in the minors most of 1952 and all of 1953 and 1954. The Cubs obtained Jones on September 30, 1954, in the trade that sent Ralph Kiner to Cleveland.

The Cubs put the 29-year-old Jones, his ever-present toothpick, and his big sweeping curve in their 1955 starting rotation. He held the Pirates hitless through eight innings on May 12. The only near-hit came in the eighth, when George Freese drove Eddie Miksis to the ivy for a leaping catch.

In the ninth inning, Jones walked the first three batters: Gene Freese (George's brother), Preston Ward, and Tom Saffell.

Jones then reared back and performed a miracle; he struck out Dick Groat, Roberto Clemente, and Frank Thomas to end the game and preserve his 4–0 no-hitter. The 2,918 fans who showed up on that threatening Thursday afternoon had a whopper of a story for the rest of their lives.

Jones's no-hitter held an additional significance. His gem was the first Wrigley Field no-hitter in 38 years, since the famed

Sam "Toothpick" Jones—a spectacular no-hitter. (National Baseball Hall of Fame Library, Cooperstown, NY)

"double no-hitter" between Jim Toney and Hippo Vaughn in May 1917. Though Wrigley had long been considered a graveyard for no-hitters, Jones's masterpiece opened a relative torrent of no-hit games at The Friendly Confines. In the next 17 seasons, pitchers tossed five no-hitters at Wrigley Field, four of them by Cubs hurlers.

- May 15, 1960   Don Cardwell vs. Cardinals   (4–0)
- August 19, 1965   Jim Maloney (Reds) vs. Cubs   (1–0)
- August 19, 1969   Ken Holtzman vs. Braves   (3–0)
- April 16, 1972   Burt Hooton vs. Phillies   (4–0)
- September 2, 1972 Milt Pappas vs. Padres   (8–0)

Sam Jones overcame many obstacles to break a baseball barrier. But he couldn't beat his final obstacle. Jones died of cancer of the neck in 1971. The 45-year-old battled the disease for nearly ten years.

12 Don Hoak struck out six times in a game on May 2, 1956, the first National Leaguer to accomplish this woeful feat. Here are Hoak's at-bats that day: first inning—called out on strikes, third inning—walk, fourth inning—single, sixth inning—strikeout, eighth inning—strikeout, 10th inning—strikeout, 13th inning—sacrifice bunt, 15th inning—strikeout, 17th inning—called out on strikes to end the game, a 6–5 loss to the Giants. Lucky for Hoak, few fans at Wrigley Field saw his final strikeout; only 2,389 diehards watched the opening pitch.

Through the 2016 season, eight major leaguers equaled Hoak's grim mark (the last being Geoff Jenkins of the Brewers in 2004). And all eight took extra innings to reach the record. Hoak's six strikeouts completed the "double-platinum sombrero" (a sombrero is three strikeouts, a golden sombrero four, and a platinum sombrero five).

Cubs reliever Lindy McDaniel owns another sorry record. He is the only pitcher to give up two walkoff grand slams in one season. Bob Aspromonte of the Houston Colt .45s took McDaniel deep in the 10th inning on June 11, 1963. Jim Hickman hit a game-winning grand slam off McDaniel on August 9th. The 7–3 Mets victory made a lucky winner of Roger Craig, who improved his record to a hard-luck 3–20.

McDaniel pitched 21 seasons, almost all in relief. He won 141 games and saved 174 more. McDaniel played for the Cubs from 1963 to 1965. He went 13–7 in 1963, his best season with the team.

The Cubs pay Jon Lester to pitch, not to hit. This gave little comfort as Lester shattered a major-league record going his first 58 at-bats without a hit. The "record breaker" came on May 27, 2015, against Max Scherzer of the Nationals. Ironically Lester smacked his longest ball in his career to date, a fly to right-center that Denard Span caught near the warning track.

Lester finally got a hit on July 6, 2015. In his 67th at-bat, Lester bounced a one-hopper that deflected off the Cardinals' John Lackey. Lester scurried to first before the shortstop retrieved the ricochet drive. That first hit soared Lester's major-league average to all of .015.

The final embarrassment is the worst of the lot, a 20-day swoon by the whole Cubs team. The Cubs opened the 1997 season with six games in Miami and Atlanta. They went 0–6 as the Marlins and Braves outscored the Cubs, 36–16. Florida and Atlanta came to Wrigley Field for two games each, and Colorado for two more. The Cubs lost them all. Their streak exploded to 0–12, a National League record for consecutive losses to start a season (in 1884 the Detroit Wolverines lost 11 games).

The Cubs lost two more in New York to extend their losing streak to 14 games. On April 20, Jose Hernandez, Kevin Orie, and Rey Sanchez knocked in runs to give Kevin Foster a 4–3 win. The Cubs finished 1997 at 68–94. That's a bad season-ending record, but the year's first three weeks were the most brutal in franchise history.

13 There are only so many possible answers to this seemingly tough question. Phil Cavarretta played parts of 20 seasons for the Cubs, the most in the Wrigley Field era. But Cavarretta ranks only fifth in number of games behind Ernie Banks, Billy Williams, Ryne Sandberg, and Ron Santo (Cavarretta managed more than 250 games he did not play in).

Banks played 19 seasons with the team and coached for two more. He also worked in the organization for decades, so he came to the park quite a bit after his playing days. Cavarretta never had a long-term post-playing career with the team.

Two other 1960s-era Cubs spent years inside Wrigley Field. Billy Williams played 16 seasons on the North Side (1959–1974). He also coached the Cubs for 15 years. But legendary third baseman Ron Santo tops the ex-player longevity list. He logged 14 years in a Cubs uniform. He also worked as radio color man from 1990 to 2010. That's 35 full seasons at Wrigley Field, the most of any former Cub.

Other men associated with the team spent decades at The Friendly Confines. P. K. Wrigley owned the Cubs for over 45 years. But outside of a few seasons in the early 1940s when he built an office inside the ballpark, Wrigley stayed away from The Friendly Confines. Some sportswriters claim the reluctant owner avoided the ballpark for years on end. He even missed big events like the 1962 All-Star Game.

Andy Lotshaw worked as a trainer for the Chicago Bears (and their predecessors, the Staleys) from 1921 to 1952. Lotshaw also served as the Cubs trainer from 1922 to 1952, when a stroke ended his career. Lotshaw logged 32 and 31 years respectively with the Bears and the Cubs.

Jack Brickhouse called Cubs games for 38 years on radio and television. He worked for WGN radio from 1940 to 1943, WBKB-TV in 1947, and WGN-TV from 1948 to 1981. Brickhouse also called Chicago Bears football games from 1953 to 1976.

Pat Pieper hawked concessions at the Cubs precursor to Wrigley Field, West Side Grounds. He followed the team to Wrigley Field in 1916. The next year Pieper worked as the

Cubs' public address announcer, and held the job until September 1974, a remarkable 59 years.

Yosh Kawano started as the assistant visiting clubhouse attendant in 1943. The Cubs promoted him to home clubhouse equipment manager, a position he held until 1999. After that he worked seven more years as a part-time visiting clubhouse assistant. That's a devoted 65 seasons at Wrigley Field!

Bobby Dorr kept Wrigley Field in top shape as head groundskeeper from 1919 until his death in 1957. Although Dorr's 38 years can't match Kawano's, Dorr worked full time, all the time. He worked during the baseball season, the football season, and right through the offseason. He and his family lived in the house adjacent to Wrigley Field (the recently renovated groundskeeper's cottage). The six-room brick house at 1053 Waveland Avenue provided direct access into the ballpark. It's not a stretch to say that Dorr entered Wrigley Field almost every day of his 38 years with the Cubs.

So who spent the most days inside Wrigley Field? Kawano's 65 seasons are eye-popping. But if Bobby Dorr spent nearly every day of his 38 years inside Wrigley Field, he'd edge out Kawano by a seeing-eye single.

14 Mike Gonzalez lived the life of a journeyman catcher. Born in Havana, Cuba, in 1890, Gonzalez played 17 years in the major leagues for six teams. He joined the Cubs on May 21, 1925, coming from the Cardinals with third baseman Howie Freigau for Waukegan native Bob O'Farrell. Gonzalez (like O'Farrell before him) backed up Gabby Hartnett. He stroked 224 hits in five years with the Cubs and produced a slash line worthy of a part-time catcher—.254/.309/.337.

Gonzalez coached, managed, and scouted longer than he played. He coached with the Cardinals and had two short stints as their manager. He scouted for Giants manager John McGraw and through his limited English coined the often-used appraisal "good field, no hit" to describe a baseball prospect.[14] Gonzalez played for, managed, and owned teams in the Cuban Leagues. He entered the Cuban Baseball Hall of Fame in 1955.

Two traits elevated Gonzalez to the big leagues: his baseball talent and his light-colored skin. The same held for a few dozen or so other light-skinned Latin ballplayers who competed in Major League Baseball before Jackie Robinson integrated the modern-day game in 1947. Some of these included 1940s Cubs like Cuban pitcher Jorge Comellas and catcher Chico Hernandez, native Puerto Rican pitcher Hi Bithorn, and Jesse Flores, a hurler from Mexico (the Cubs' Bithorn and Hernandez made up the first all-Latin major-league battery on April 27, 1942). Darker-skinned Latin ballplayers like Minnie Minoso and Roberto Clemente fell under baseball's unwritten ban on black athletes. They didn't play major-league baseball before Robinson broke the color barrier.

Times change. The 2016 Cubs featured seven Latin players, more than a fourth of their roster. It seems strange today to talk about the novelty of a Latin major-league ballplayer, but at one time, Latin players (at least light-skinned ones) were unique.

15 The Cubs who answer this question played after at least two of the three big RBI men—Ernie Banks, Ron Santo, and Billy Williams—left the team. Banks retired in 1971, Santo left after the 1973 season, and Williams lasted through 1974.

Williams split 1974 between first base and left field. He drove in 68 runs. Outfielder Jerry Morales patrolled left and center field and knocked in 82 runs. Jose Cardenal played right field and drove in 72. That's the first time two Latin ballplayers led the Cubs in RBIs.

Morales paced the team with 91 RBIs the following year. Second baseman Manny Trillo drove in 70, and Cardenal 68. Three Latin players led the Cubs in RBIs in 1975.

Jerry Morales hailed from Puerto Rico. He bantered around the San Diego Padres system before he came to the Cubs in 1973 for aging second baseman Glenn Beckert. Morales spent seven years in Chicago over two stretches: 1974–1977 and 1981–1983. He stroked 711 hits and drove in 375 runs.

The native Cuban Cardenal spent 18 years in the big leagues and wandered around like a nomad. Before coming to the Cubs in 1972, he played for the Giants, Angels, Indians, Cardinals, and Brewers. But Cardenal had his best six years with the Cubs. He produced four consecutive .800-plus OPS seasons and stole 129 bases. His basepath exploits produced one of Cardenal's lasting images—his Cubs cap flying off his enormous afro as he ran.

Cardenal had a reputation as a flake, and he entertainingly lived up to it. He once missed a spring training game because a cricket kept him awake. He also missed a game because his eyelid got stuck. Cardenal played a violin and said he nibbled on the ivy. He filled the team with necessary lightheartedness, but he played hard. The staid Cubs hadn't seen anything like Cardenal for quite some time, and fans loved him.

Manny Trillo also spent two tours of duty with the Cubs: 1975–1978 and 1986–1989. The native Venezuelan first came to the Cubs in the Billy Williams trade. After four years he went to Philadelphia, won three Gold Glove Awards, and helped the Phillies to the 1980 World Series. Trillo rejoined the Cubs and played all the infield positions in a reserve role.

The year 1975 marked the first great Latin invasion of the Cubs. In addition to Morales, Cardenal, and Trillo, Cuban reliever Oscar Zamora pitched in 52 games, and Puerto Rican shortstop Dave Rosello saw 71 plate appearances. The Cubs' "Latin Five" wouldn't be equaled until 1993, when six Latin ballplayers graced the Cubs roster: Rey Sanchez, Candy Maldonado, and Jose Guzman from Puerto Rico; and Sammy Sosa, Jose Bautista, and Jose Vizcaino from the Dominican Republic.

16 The youngest Cubs pitcher ever, Dick Ellsworth, started the annual exhibition game against the White Sox at Comiskey Park on June 16, 1958. Just a week out of high school, the 18-year-old whiz shutout the Pale Hose on four hits. Manager Bob Scheffing started Ellsworth six days later in Cincinnati. The Reds roughed him up, and the Cubs sent him down to the minors.

Ellsworth reappeared in 1960 as a 20-year-old and stayed with the Cubs through 1966. During the 1960s, he led the team in starts (235), wins (84), complete games (71), and innings (1,611). But Ellsworth endured a roller coaster career. He lost 20 games in 1962, won 22 in 1963, and lost 22 more in 1966. In 12 years with the Cubs, Phillies, Red Sox, Indians, and Brewers, he won 115 games.

The Cubs brought up nine teenagers between 1958 and 1969. That would never happen today. The adage of "get them on the field to see what they can do" is anathema as clubs worry about a young player's psyche. Even prized prospects need success at one level before they move to another. But in Ellsworth's day management took risks to jolt a weak lineup or excite the dwindling fan base. How rare are major-league teenagers? The last Cubs teenager was Oscar Gamble in 1969.

The Cubs' top five winners in the 1960s—

- Dick Ellsworth   84
- Fergie Jenkins   67
- Larry Jackson   52
- Bob Buhl   51
- Bill Hands   51

Dick Ellsworth—a Cubs pitching prodigy. (National Baseball Hall of Fame Library, Cooperstown, NY)

The Cubs' top winner for each decade—

- 1870s   Terry Larkin   113
- 1880s   Larry Corcoran   252
- 1890s   Bill Hutchinson   284
- 1900s   Mordecai Brown   151
- 1910s   Hippo Vaughn   146
- 1920s   Grover Alexander   136
- 1930s   Bill Lee, Lon Warneke   110
- 1940s   Claude Passeau   111
- 1950s   Bob Rush   95
- 1960s   Dick Ellsworth   84
- 1970s   Rick Reuschel   114
- 1980s   Rick Sutcliffe   76
- 1990s   Steve Trachsel   60
- 2000s   Carlos Zambrano   105

17 During the 1960s and early 1970s, the Cubs habitually picked up old ballplayers. Management hoped to squeeze one bit of usefulness from their almost cooked bats or arms. Former All-Star-caliber players like Richie Ashburn, Lew Burdette, Harvey Kuenn, Robin Roberts, Don Larsen, Juan Pizarro, and Rico Carty all spent part of their late careers with the North Siders. But the oldest Cub? That's Hoyt Wilhelm.

On September 21, 1970, with a shorn bullpen and a team two games behind the Pirates with 10 to play, the Cubs plucked the 47-year-old knuckleballer off waivers. Wilhelm pitched poorly in two of three relief appearances. Before the end of the year, the Cubs traded Wilhelm back to the Braves for first baseman Hal Breeden.

Wilhelm played two more seasons before retiring at a Methuselah-like 49 years old. He won 143 games, most of them in relief. Wilhelm entered the National Baseball Hall of Fame in 1985, the first relief pitcher to get that honor. And while Wilhelm pitched in a then major-league record 1,070 games, just three of them came on the Cubs. But he is the oldest Cub in history.

Ballplayers over 40 years old, like teenagers, are uncommon today. With burgeoning salaries there's less incentive for older players to lengthen careers. So as sure as a knuckleball has a mind of its own, Wilhelm's Cubs record is safe for the foreseeable future.

18 Murphy's Bleachers occupies the greatest piece of real estate in Major League Baseball—a stone's throw from the legendary Wrigley Field bleachers. Cubs fans made Murphy's a pre- and postgame tradition for decades. But the famous watering hole at 3655 N. Sheffield Avenue has a long history that predates the "Murphy's" name.

Murphy's Bleachers sits on a former empty lot. A portable hot dog stand named "Ernie's Bleachers" stood there in the 1930s. Ernie built a brick building on the property in 1940. A few years later Ernie sold the bar and it became "J.B.'s." J. B. sold it back to Ernie, and in 1962, Ray and Marge Meyer took it over.

Ray's Bleachers stumbled on immortality. The place screamed simplicity: 12 barstools, a pinball machine, and a pool table with a plywood covering. But the Meyers got lucky. The previously moribund Cubs came alive in 1967, finishing third in the 10-team National League. Fans returned to Wrigley Field, and the little bar achieved cult status as the home of the famous "Bleacher Bums."

When they weren't at Ray's, a dozen or so regulars hung out in the bleachers. They played catch with the players before the game and verbally abused the opposition. One had a bugle. An older couple named Ma and Big Daddy Barker showed up one day with signs painted on bedsheets. One had a hole in the middle, surrounded by the words, "Hit the Bleacher Bum." The "kids" stuck their heads through the opening. When the media visited Wrigley Field to document the revived Cubs, a Chicago newspaper ran a photo of the shenanigans. The "Bleacher Bums" name went mainstream.

As the team competed in 1968 and improved in 1969, the "Bums," with their chants and their antics, became integral to the Wrigley Field scene. They were loud, obnoxious, and a little edgy, perfect for the counter-culture revolution of the late-1960s. The Bleacher Bums shared their notoriety with the place many of them visited before and after Wrigley Field—Ray's Bleachers.

As the "Cub Power" era faded in the early 1970s, and the young Bleacher Bums became responsible adults and left Wrigley Field, Ray's Bleachers lost its cache. Ray and Marge Meyer sold the bar in 1980. Ray died in 1985 and is buried in Graceland Cemetery, just a few blocks north of his old bar.

Jim Murphy purchased the bar in 1980 and renamed it "Murphy's Bleachers." Murphy held more business chops than Ray Meyer. He maximized the bar's potential, adding a beer garden, Irish bar, an enclosed grill, an upper deck party room, and a rooftop pavilion. It became an institution and tourist attraction—recession proof and popular no matter what the Cubs were doing.

Although Murphy made his living off Cubs fans, he led the early-21st-century fight against Wrigley Field bleacher expansion as the president of the Wrigley Field Rooftop Owners Association and the Lake View Neighbors. Mr. Murphy died at 54 years old in January 2003. The city dedicated a portion of Waveland Avenue near the ballpark, naming it "Honorable Jim Murphy Way."

19 You don't have to be a superstar to write yourself into the record books. Take the curious career of Doug Dascenzo. The Cubs took the switch-hitting outfielder in the 12th round of the 1985 amateur draft. Dascenzo reached the Cubs in a 1998 late-season call-up. He stroked three hits in his first game on September 2, a Cubs record (later equaled by Kosuke Fukudome in 2008 and Junior Lake in 2013). Dascenzo didn't commit an error that game and went 241 consecutive games without an error to start his career. That broke a major-league record.

But the 5'7" left-hander's greatest fame comes from his relief pitching prowess. Manager Don Zimmer sent Dascenzo to the mound during four blowouts in 1990 and 1991. And Dascenzo did pretty well. He appeared in the eighth or ninth innings of games the Cubs trailed 19–6, 13–5, 14–5, and 13–1. He threw five innings and gave up no runs on just two hits. That's one of the best career pitching efforts in major-league history.

Dascenzo played five years with the Cubs as a reserve outfielder and a late-inning defensive specialist. He hit .240/.301/.300. He finished up his career with the Rangers and the Padres. After his playing days, he coached and managed in the Padres and Braves organizations, worked as the Braves third base coach, and now serves as an outfielder coach with the Cubs.

Doug Dascenzo proved you don't have to be a hotshot to make a name for yourself. He's just a blip on the radar of Cubs history, but his unique contributions made him a cult hero at Wrigley Field, when the likes of Andre Dawson and Ryne Sandberg took most of the headlines.

20 The 2012 Cubs went 61–101, just the third time they lost more than 100 games in franchise history (they had identical 59–103 records in 1962 and 1966). The Cubs starters had little success that year. Jeff Samardzija went 9–13, Travis Wood 6–13, Chris Volstead 3–12, and Justin Germano 2–10. Only Paul Maholm pulled off a winning record at 9–6. The Cubs traded him to the Braves on July 30.

The Cubs relievers didn't fare much better. But James Russell was an outlier, going 7–1. Russell pitched well. He appeared in 77 games in relief and posted a respectable 3.25 ERA and a 1.298 WHIP. But there's no way to explain his odd won-loss record. It's especially peculiar when you examine his 2013 record. That year the Cubs were bad again, but won five more games. Russell put up similar numbers (3.59 ERA, 1.215 WHIP), but nearly reversed his record, going 1–6. It's just unexplainable.

Virtually all pitchers before World War II both started and relieved. But the better pitchers started more, and the lesser ones relieved more. The only Cubs pitcher before World War II to relieve exclusively was Jack Russell. Russell threw in 81 games with the Cubs in 1938 and 1939, all in relief. He went 10–4.

After World War II, the Cubs (and most other teams) designated one or two pitchers per year as exclusive relievers. Chicagoan Emil Kush pitched in relief in 1947 and 1948. An old knuckleballer named Dutch Leonard took relief honors from 1950 to 1953. Converted center fielder Hal Jeffcoat pitched relief in 1954 and 1955. That led to Turk Lown from 1954 to 1957, "Everyday" Don Elston from 1958 to 1964, and Lindy McDaniel in 1963 and 1964.

Relief specialists became common in the 1960s. And with them came some irrational yearly records. Lindy McDaniel went 13–7 with the 1963 Cubs. He slipped to just 1–7 in 1964. The star-crossed 1969 Cubs team featured closer Phil Regan. The "Vulture" spun a 12–6 record. He went just 5–9 in 1970. But few relievers fluctuated their yearly records like Dick Tidrow. The Cubs set-up man went 11–5 in 1979, 3–10 in 1981, and 8–3 in 1982.

Strange reliever numbers continued. The great Lee Smith led the National League with 29 saves in 1983. He posted a remarkable 1.65 ERA and a tiny 1.074 WHIP. Yet he went just 4–10. Smith won nine games in relief in 1986, tying for the team lead with starter Scott Sanderson. He went 4–10 once again in 1987. Ryan Dempster saved 52 games in 2006 and 2007. But his record limped along at 3–16. Again—unexplainable.

This finally brings us to Jason Motte. The bearded reliever seemingly chalked up an undistinguished 2015 season (he's most noted for leading the Cubs bullpen in rhythmic claps to walk-up songs). But Motte etched an 8–1 record.

Relief pitching is a tricky business. It's also an unstable one; records can fluctuate wildly. Perhaps that's why relievers come and go. It's also another reason we easily remember Dizzy Dean but not Jack Russell, Fergie Jenkins but not Phil Regan, and Rick Reuschel but not Dick Tidrow.

21 The 1965 Cubs stunk. They finished the year 72–90, one in a string of 20 straight years in the second division (the bottom half of the eight- or ten-team National League).

Even though that stretch (1947–1966) showcased lots of bad baseball, no one imagined the Cubs being no-hit twice during any of those seasons. But that's what happened in 1965. On August 19 at Wrigley Field, the Reds' Jim Maloney tossed an incomparable 10-inning no-hitter. Maloney struck out 12, walked 10, and threw an arm-throbbing 187 pitches. Just 21 days later on September 9, Sandy Koufax tossed a perfect game against the Cubs at Dodger Stadium. The two no-hitters marked only the fourth time since 1900 that one team lost two no-hitters in the same season.

As the seasons unfolded toward the end of the 1960s, through the mediocre 1970s, past the up-and-down 1980s, and into the next century, it seemed logical someone would no-hit the Cubs. But it never happened. There were close calls. On July 9, 1969, light-hitting Jim Qualls broke up Tom Seaver's perfect game in the ninth inning. Ernie Banks ended Gary Gentry's May 13, 1970, no-hit bid with an eighth-inning single. And on April 10, 1997, third baseman Dave Hansen squibbed a ninth-inning infield hit to spoil Alex Fernandez's no-hit effort. Pitchers one-hit the Cubs 25 times between September 10, 1965, and July 24, 2015.

On July 25, 2015, the Phillies' Cole Hamels no-hit the Cubs into the ninth inning. Would a savior appear for the Cubs, like Qualls, Banks, or Hansen? Kris Bryant batted with two outs. He launched a deep fly to center field. Odubel Herrera ran back to the ivy, then lunged forward. He landed in a heap, as warning-track dirt wafted around him. But he held the ball in his glove; the streak ended. The Cubs went 7,920 games without being no-hit. That's nearly 50 years, the longest stretch in major-league history.

With the Cubs streak gone, the longest belonged to the Reds, whose streak began on June 24, 1970. Jake Arrieta went up against the Reds the following spring, on April 21, 2016. He and the Cubs were lights out that night in Cincinnati. Arrieta threw a 16–0 no-hitter, his second in 15 starts. The Cubs stopped the Reds' streak at 7,109 games.

The Cubs "no no-hit" record is safe. The current streak belongs to the A's. They've gone just over 4,000 games without being no-hit. If they continue their streak, they'll pass the Cubs mark on or around 2040.

22 It takes a special player to pinch-hit. It's difficult to come off the bench and deliver in the clutch. Statistics show that batters who start a game succeed more than they would as pinch-hitters. Starting hitters had this slash line in 2005— .254/.319/.395. But as pinch-hitters the same batters hit just .228/.306/.336.[15]

Here are the Cubs' top five pinch-hitters. All batted left-handed.

- Dwight Smith   1989–1993   50 pinch hits

Smith finished second for the 1989 National League Rookie of the Year Award behind teammate Jerome Walton. He hit .323 with 111 hits in 1989, but he subbed the rest of his career. Smith hit .266 as a pinch-hitter.

- Larry Biittner   1976–1980   46 pinch hits

The 14-year veteran had his best seasons in Chicago. Biittner played first base and outfield, and often subbed for ailing Bill Buckner. His career highlights include pitching (poorly) in the second game of a 1977 July 4th doubleheader, and clubbing a walkoff home run to win the 1978 home opener.

- Thad Bosley   1983–1986   46 pinch hits

Another 14-year veteran, Bosley got 345 pinch-hitting opportunities, and hit .283 in that role. Bosley played for the Cubs, Angels, White Sox, Brewers, Mariners, Royals, and Rangers.

- Phil Cavarretta   1934–1953   46 pinch hits

A high number of Cavarretta's pinch-hit opportunities came during his time as player-manager (32 in 1951, 24 in 1952, and 25 in 1953).

- Bob Will   1957–1958, 1960–1963   46 pinch hits

A local kid from suburban Berwyn, Will rode an up-and-down career with the Cubs: up with the Cubs in 1957, down in the minors for most of 1958 and all of 1959, up with the Cubs in 1960 and 1961, back in the minors for most of 1962 and 1963.

23 Long home runs at Wrigley differ from those at other ball-parks. Huge home runs land in the second or the third decks in most stadiums. Tape-measure shots at Wrigley Field are more interesting—they land on streets, off buildings, or even on the buildings' roofs.

Most long Wrigley Field home runs clear Waveland and Sheffield Avenues. The most prodigious land on Kenmore Avenue, perpendicular to and beyond Waveland Avenue in left field.

Here are the five longest home runs to leave Wrigley Field (in chronological order).

- Roberto Clemente (Pirates) May 17, 1959, off Bill Henry (74 degrees, variable south wind)

Batters blasted 10 home runs during this doubleheader. Clemente hit the last one, in the ninth inning of the second game. His line shot departed the park to the left of the scoreboard. Recent testimony by a ballhawk who saw it claimed the ball short-hopped the curb on the north side of Waveland Avenue. If true, it means the center field shot traveled well over 500 feet on a fly.

- Joe Adcock (Braves) September 3, 1961, off Jim Brewer (85 degrees, strong west wind)

Adcock's drive struck the building at 3703 N. Kenmore. Only Dave Kingman hit a building further north on Kenmore Avenue.

- Dave Kingman (Mets) April 14, 1976, off Tom Dettore (80 degrees, strong southwest wind)

On the warmest day to date in 1976, Kingman crushed the longest ball to date at Wrigley Field. His drive bounced near the third house up Kenmore Avenue (3705 Kenmore). It traveled about 530 feet, one of the longest in major-league history.

- Dave Kingman (vs. Phillies) May 17, 1979, off Doug Bird (78 degrees, 18 mph south wind)

When the Phillies outlasted the Cubs in the 23–22 slugfest, the teams combined for a record-tying 11 home runs. Dave Kingman struck three. His fourth-inning bazooka shot hit the Kenmore Avenue house where he landed one three years earlier. Kingman sent another home run off a Waveland Avenue building, hitting two of the park's longer home runs in one afternoon.

Dave Kingman—the Cubs' big hitter of the late-1970s. (National Baseball Hall of Fame Library, Cooperstown, NY)

- Sammy Sosa (vs. Brewers) June 24, 2003, off Luis Vizcaino (90 degrees, south wind)

Sosa hit more tape-measure home runs than anyone at Wrigley Field. This fifth-inning clout landed in the middle of Kenmore Avenue, a GPS-measured 536 feet. Veteran ballhawks claimed that Sosa's bested Kingman's two long shots by a few feet.

*   In case you're wondering . . . On May 11, 2000, Glenallen Hill drove a ball onto the roof of 1032 Waveland Avenue. It traveled about 500 feet. It was a drive of epic proportions, but not one of the five longest in Wrigley Field history.

24 This is subjective, but this answer recognizes a few position players whose contributions might otherwise have been missed. Here are three worthy candidates.

- Aramis Ramirez came from the Pirates in 2003. That year he helped the Cubs to the National League Championship Series. Ramirez played nine seasons on the North Side and hit 239 home runs with a slash line of .294/.356/.531, and a .887 OPS. Ramirez filled a longtime void as the Cubs' best offensive third baseman between Ron Santo and Kris Bryant.

Ramirez's greatest moment in a Cubs uniform occurred on June 29, 2007. With the Cubs losing 5–4 to the Brewers in the last of the ninth inning, Ramirez cracked a two-run walkoff blast against Francisco Cordero. The Cubs trailed the Brewers by 6½ games before Ramirez's smash. After the walkoff blast, they went on a tear and won the National League Central title.

- Bill Nicholson led the Cubs in home runs eight straight seasons (1940–1947). The right fielder twice led the league in home runs and RBIs (in 1943 and 1944), and hit 235 home runs from 1939 to 1948. Nicholson appeared in four All-Star Games and twice finished in the top five for the National League Most Valuable Player Award.

Nicholson lost the 1944 National League Most Valuable Player Award to the Cardinals' Marty Marion by one vote. Nicholson led the league in home runs, drove in 122 RBIs, had a 6.0 WAR, and a .935 OPS. Marion hit just .267 with six home runs and a .686 OPS. Marion compiled a 4.7 WAR but only 1.1 of it came on offense. Marion won because of his defensive work at shortstop and the Cardinals' third-straight pennant. Had the award been given out today, with the advanced metrics available to sportswriters, Nicholson certainly would have won.

- Stan Hack joined the Cubs in 1932 as a 22-year-old rookie. He played his whole 16-year career with the team and spent eight years as leadoff hitter. The third baseman twice led the league in hits and twice more in stolen bases. He appeared in four All-Star Games. When he retired in 1947, he had compiled a slew of commendable statistics: a .301 batting average, 2,193 hits, a .394 on-base percentage, and five years of at least 4.9 offensive WAR. With the exception of Sammy Sosa, Hack has the highest career WAR (52.5) of any Cub not in the Hall of Fame.

Old-time fans fondly remember Hack. He managed the Cubs from 1954 to 1956 but had less success than in his playing days. His on-field excellence and winning personality, however, made him a very popular Cub in his day. But Hack is all but forgotten, especially when compared to Hall of Fame teammates like Gabby Hartnett. Hack is arguably the most underrated and underappreciated player in Cubs history.

4

HOME RUNS LEVEL

(Answers begin on page 139.)

You have to know your stuff to answer these. But even if you have no clue, there are lots of interesting stories. Ballparks before Wrigley Field? First-bat home runs? A Cub who played for the Packers? You may need to call in your closer. It's getting hot out there!

1. What Cub threw three no-hitters?
2. Where did the team play before Wrigley Field?
3. Which came first? The Waveland Avenue firehouse or Wrigley Field?
4. Who hit the Cubs' first postseason home run?
5. Who was Charlie Hollocher?
6. Who were Mandy Brooks and Bob Speake?
7. Which Cub produced 20- and 27-game hitting streaks in the same season?
8. When did the Cubs first draw a million fans in a season?
9. Who was Hal Carlson?
10. Name the player who became the first major leaguer to not hit into a double play all year, the first to homer from both sides of the plate in a game, and the first Cub to homer at the All-Star Game?
11. What fan favorite's debut occurred in front of the smallest crowd in Wrigley Field history?
12. Which Cubs uniform number was worn by the most future Hall of Famers?
13. Name two of the five Cubs pitchers to smoke two home runs in a game?
14. Name four of the eight Cubs to homer in their first major-league at-bat.
15. Which former Cubs pitcher fashioned a 23–3 record against the North Siders?
16. Who is the only Cub to also play for the Green Bay Packers?

17. Who was Robert Whitlow, and what does his hiring tell us about Cubs owner, P. K. Wrigley?

18. Which Cubs outfielder had the highest single-game Win Probability Added (WPA) in team history?

19. Only once did the Cubs pick first in the annual draft. What was the year, and who did they draft?

20. The Cubs employed 10 left-handed pitchers during the 2000 season. Name four of them.

21. Which Cubs team scored the most runs on Opening Day?

22. Who holds the Cubs at-bats record for a season? Hint— he played only one year with the team.

23. Which pitcher holds the Cubs record for the fewest allowed hits per nine innings, and most strikeouts per nine innings?

24. Name seven of the 14 Cubs whose last name begins with the letter Z.

HOME RUNS LEVEL ANSWERS

1 Ken Holtzman and Jake Arrieta tossed two no-hitters. Three Finger Brown and Hippo Vaughn have five one-hitters apiece. But three no-hitters?

White Stockings pitcher Larry Corcoran went 43–14 in 1880, one of the greatest rookie seasons in baseball history. The 5'3", 127-pound Corcoran threw an elbow-rattling 536 innings that year. His brilliance led the White Stockings to a 35–3 start, and they ran away with the National League pennant.

Corcoran's next four seasons (1881–1884) weren't bad either: 31–14, 27–12, 34–20, and 35–23. He helped the White Stockings to pennants in 1881 and 1882. From 1880 to 1885 Corcoran dazzled with a 175–85 record. But he's most noted for tossing three no-hitters, the first major leaguer to do so.

- August 19, 1880—Corcoran no-hit the Boston Red Caps, 6–0. It's just the fourth no-hitter in the National League's five-year history.
- September 20, 1882—Corcoran turned the trick again with a 5–0 whitewashing versus Worcester. It was the last home game of the season, and Corcoran became the first man to throw two major-league no-hitters.
- June 27, 1884—Corcoran threw his third no-hitter, a record that stood until Sandy Koufax tossed his fourth, against the Cubs in 1965. Corcoran beat the Providence Grays, the eventual league champs, 6–0. Two weeks before on June 16,

Corcoran became the first and only pitcher to throw with both hands in a game. He tossed a portion of four innings left-handed because of a sore finger on his right hand.[16]

The White Stockings rode Corcoran hard and he developed arm troubles. His delicate shoulder finally shut down in 1885, and the White Stockings released him. He pitched seven more games the next two and a half seasons with New York, Washington, and Indianapolis, and retired for good in 1887. Corcoran died on October 14, 1891, from Bright's disease, a kidney ailment. He was just 32 years old.

2 The Chicago Cubs have called Wrigley Field home since 1916. But the Chicago Nationals moved a lot before then, playing in five home ballparks in 40 years. Here is a list of their ballparks in chronological order:

- 1876–1877   23rd Street Grounds

The White Stockings inaugurated the National Association in 1871. Their first ballpark burned down that year during the Great Chicago Fire. They resumed play in 1874 when they built a ballpark at 23rd and South Federal Street, east of present-day Chinatown. The White Stockings played there two seasons as a National Association team and two more when they joined the National League in 1876. They won the National League title that first season.

- 1878–1884   Lake Front Park

The White Stockings moved to near Michigan Avenue and Randolph Street, ironically on what is now Wrigley Square in

Millennium Park. They renovated the ballpark in 1883, doubling capacity and shortening the dimensions—180 feet to the left field wall, the shortest in major-league history. Balls stroked over the left field wall were ground-rule doubles in 1883, but home runs in 1884. It skyrocketed the White Stockings' home-run total those two years from 13 to 142. The White Stockings won National League titles in 1880, 1881, and 1882.

- 1885–1891   Westside Park

The team moved west to Congress Parkway and South Loomis Street, a block from the present-day UIC Pavilion. The area was residential, and neighbors protested the park's construction. That's why it opened a month later than scheduled. The field was long and narrow, surrounded by a bicycle track, a popular sport at the time. The White Stockings won National League titles in 1885 and 1886.

- 1891–1893   Southside Park

A temporary repurposed home for just parts of three seasons, it earlier housed the Chicago team in the short-lived Players' League (1890). The park stood at 35th and South Wentworth, just east of what would be the original Comiskey Park. The team used the park part-time in 1891, full-time in 1892, and part-time again in 1893, when they split the season between South Side Park and West Side Grounds.

- 1893–1915   West Side Grounds

The last of the team's wooden parks, the place almost burned down during a game in 1894. Located on what is now Taylor

Street and South Wolcott, fans came via trains that followed a path similar to the present-day Pink Line and exited at Polk Street, just a block away. The Cubs stayed here until they moved to Clark and Addison Streets in 1916. The University of Illinois Medical Center sits on the old ballpark property.

3 We know the Chi-Feds built Wrigley Field as Weeghman Park in 1914. But what about the fire station across the street? It seems like a bad idea to build the station next to a ballpark. We've seen fire trucks caught in ballpark traffic and the mass of humanity on Waveland Avenue before and after games. So what is it? Was the firehouse there before the ballpark? Or the ballpark there before the firehouse?

The Engine 78 firehouse stands at 1052 W. Waveland Avenue, across from Wrigley Field's left field corner. The brick building dates to 1915, one year newer than Wrigley Field. But that's not the first firehouse on that site. The Chicago Fire Department relocated a wood building there in 1894, just as families and businesses developed the area. Many buildings in the neighborhood, including those on Sheffield Avenue across from the right field wall, date from the late 1880s to the mid-1890s.

The Chicago Fire Department built the 1915 brick building without a hayloft for horse-drawn fire wagons. That means it was among the first to use motorized vehicles exclusively.

The firefighters of Engine 78 developed a deep-seated relationship with the Cubs and Wrigley Field. They've been inside the ballpark numerous times to put out small fires and take injured ballplayers to the hospital. Before and during games they sit outside the station and greet fans. The fire hydrant adjacent to the station has a spigot that acts as a drinking fountain on game days. Legend has it that fans who drink from the fountain bring the Cubs good luck.

4 Since the modern-day World Series began in 1903, the Cubs have appeared in postseason play 18 times through 2016. The team's first five appearances (1906, 1907, 1908, 1910, and 1918) occurred during the so-called Dead Ball Era, when pitching, defense, and "small ball" dominated.

During these five World Series (and 27 games), the Cubs hit only one home run. Shortstop Joe Tinker struck a blow off the Tigers' "Wild Bill" Donovan in Game 2 of the 1908 World Series at West Side Grounds. Donovan held the Cubs to just one hit through seven innings. But Solly Hofman's eighth-inning bunt single brought Tinker to the plate. The *New York Times* described the home run: "There was an unusual amount of energy behind the hit, and it sailed high and clear into the stand in right field. Tinker, preceded by Hofman, trotted around the circuit amidst the first real cheering of the game. Horns were blown, bells rung, and throats strained to increase the ovation."[17] The Cubs won the game, 6–1. They'd win the series four games to one, their second-straight World Series title.

Tinker's home run was unusual. It was the only home run of the five-game series and the first World Series home run in five years. His blast started an explosion of six runs, the most runs the Cubs scored in one inning of any World Series game in their history.

Joe Tinker mostly blasted teams with his defense. Five times Tinker led the National League in defensive WAR, and he compiled a 34.3 career defensive WAR, the fifth best in major-league history. Tinker hit just 28 home runs in 12 years on the Cubs. But while dwarfed historically by sluggers like Hack Wilson, Ernie Banks, and Sammy Sosa, the defensive specialist hit one of the most important home runs in Cubs World Series history.

After Tinker retired as a full-time player, he served as a player-manager for the 1913 Reds, the 1914–1915 Chicago Federals, and the 1916 Cubs. He entered the National Baseball Hall of Fame with his famous double play cohorts, Johnny Evers and Frank Chance, in 1946. Tinker died in 1948 at 68 years old.

5 Little Charlie Hollocher played big. The 5'7" shortstop came out of nowhere as one of the top rookies in 1918. He averaged .316, compiled a 5.0 WAR, and led the league in hits and total bases. Hollocher stole 26 bases and provided the missing spark that drove the Cubs to the 1918 pennant.

Hollocher missed large stretches of the 1920 season with a mysterious stomach ailment. He stopped playing altogether in mid-August, and doctors couldn't diagnose his problem. He returned to his excellent form in 1921 and 1922. During the latter season, he socked 201 hits, batted .340, and compiled a .847 OPS, unusual for a man who hit all of three home runs.

Hollocher's ailment reappeared after the 1922 season. He came back to the Cubs in May 1923 and hit .342. But Hollocher took himself out of the lineup again on August 3. He did not return until May 1924 and he struggled. He quit the team in August 1924 and never played major-league baseball again.

Specialists never determined what ailed Charlie Hollocher, or why he might have sabotaged his budding career. He suffered from depression, and many speculated that a mental

Charlie Hollocher. (Photo Courtesy of the Library of Congress)

condition, and not a physical problem, led to his demise. Hollocher bounced around after that (he scouted for the Cubs for a short time). But on August 14, 1940, the recently married 44-year-old took his own life. No one knew why.

6 Brooks and Speake defined "flash in the pan."

The struggling 1925 Cubs looked for offense. They shopped the minor leagues and plucked Mandy Brooks from Columbus of the American Association on May 26, 1925. The 5'9", 165-pound outfielder would exemplify the most extreme example of "feast to famine" in Cubs history.

Brooks caught fire immediately and his June produced an offensive start unseen before or since by a Cubs rookie. Brooks stroked 15 multi-hit games that month and batted .408. He rattled ten doubles, four triples, and nine home runs; his OPS was a staggering 1.280. Brooks peaked on June 21 at Cubs Park. He poked a two-run game-winning home run off Art Decatur of the Phillies for a 3–2 Cubs victory. As Brooks circled the bases, he barreled his way through throngs of fans who rushed the field to celebrate.

But Brooks came back to Earth. He hit a paltry .198 in July. He improved a bit in August but played sparingly thereafter. The Cubs picked up Hack Wilson in 1926. Brooks got only 48 at-bats and hit just .188. He returned to the minors on June 22, 1926, and never played major-league baseball again.

Thirty years after Mandy Brooks's magnificent June, a 24-year-old rookie staged a sensational May. Bob Speake rode the bench early in the 1955 season. On May 1, manager Stan Hack summoned Speake to left field to replace the team's ailing slugger, Hank Sauer.

The left-handed Speake surprised everyone when he hit just like Sauer. He mashed his first major-league home run on May 5, a massive drive over the right field roof at the Polo Grounds. His two-run extra-inning clout helped the Cubs clip the Braves 4–2 on May 20. And on May 30, he homered in the ninth inning and singled in a run in the 10th as the Cubs won the first game of two against the Cardinals. He drilled a homer in the 11th inning of the nightcap to complete the sweep.

Speake knocked 10 home runs and 29 RBIs for the month, good for a .282 average and a 1.098 OPS. His startling power numbers led the Cubs to a 27–17 record, second place behind the Dodgers. Speake even led all National League left fielders in early All-Star Game voting.

But like Brooks before him, Speake's stardom lasted just a month. He hit a forgettable .149 in June and homered only once. As both Speake and the Cubs swooned, he was back on the bench before the Fourth of July.

Speake's career continued to yo-yo. He spent 1956 on the Cubs' Triple-A Los Angeles team. He resurfaced in 1957 and belted 16 home runs for the Cubs, but hit only .232. On April 3, 1958, the Cubs traded Speake to the Giants for Bobby Thomson. Speake had an insignificant role on two Giants teams and didn't play major-league ball after 1959.

Mandy Brooks and Bob Speake came, they played, and they soon went home.

7 Bill Dahlen owns the longest hitting streak by a Chicago National. He compiled a 42-game streak in 1894. Dahlen's is the fourth longest in major-league history, behind Joe DiMaggio, Wee Willie Keeler, and Pete Rose. Rookie Jerome Walton owns the longest Cubs hitting streak since 1900. He hit in 30 straight games in 1989.

Only two Cubs since 1900 have more than one hitting streak of at least 20 games. Second baseman Glenn Beckert had three. Beckert compiled streaks of 20 games in 1966, 27 games in 1968, and 26 games in 1973. Beckert was the prototype of the long-streak hitter: He hit for average, had decent speed, and seldom struck out (Beckert is the 42nd toughest batter to strike out in major-league history). Beckert was among the last of a breed—a batter who choked-up and controlled where the ball went, not like the modern-day batter who swings from his heels.

Slugger Hack Wilson had little in common with Beckert, but had four long hitting streaks: 25 games in 1927, 20 games and 27 games in 1929, and 22 games in 1930. Standing just 5'6" and weighing at least 220 pounds, the stubby-looking

Wilson looked like nobody else in the game. And he hit like no one outside of Babe Ruth. He overpowered the opposition and hit home runs in bunches.

Wilson led the National League in home runs four times. He hit 39 home runs in 1929 and posted an incredible slash line of .345/.425/.618. The following year he did even better: .356/.454/.723. Wilson rocked 56 home runs in 1930 and drove in 191 runs, still the most in major-league history.

Wilson was arguably the most electrifying player in Cubs history, both on and off the field. Beyond his offensive excellence between the foul lines, Wilson drank heavily, he fought with opposing players, and he even battled with fans. His infamous fisticuffs with a milkman at Wrigley Field stole headlines for days. Hack Wilson—magnificently talented and tremendously fascinating. Fans couldn't get enough of him.

But Wilson's fire burnt out quickly. After his stellar 1930 season, he partied too much, he lost his batting eye, and he got into one last brawl in a train station. Though Wilson lasted only six years with the Cubs, he built a legacy unrivaled in team history.

8 If you think about this for a while, it adds up. The 1925 Cubs finished in last place for the first time in the franchise's 50-year history. Disheartened

Hack Wilson—the most dynamic Cub ever. (National Baseball Hall of Fame Library, Cooperstown, NY)

Cubs fans looked for someone, anyone to ignite the team. They got a spark from the aforementioned Hack Wilson.

The team's fiery new left fielder led the league in home runs. His 21 longballs included clutch drives, dramatic game-winners, and mammoth shots never before seen at Wrigley Field. Fans ate it up and Wilson supplanted Grover Cleveland Alexander as the most popular Cub. With Wilson leading the resurgence, the Cubs' 1926 attendance increased by over 250,000 to a franchise-record 885,063. Fans often filled Cubs Park to capacity; it needed more seats.

The team built the upper deck after the 1926 season. But they finished only the third-base half because of a snowstorm and steel shipment delays. The new seats propelled the Cubs to another attendance record—1,159,168 fans, the first one million or more attendance in team history.

The Cubs completed the upper deck project after the 1927 season. The exciting team continued winning and their attendance reached a major-league record 1,485,166 in 1929, the year the Cubs won the National League pennant. That record held until the 1946 Yankees drew over two million.

The winning Cubs of the late 1920s drew better than any major-league team before them. Give a nod to Hack Wilson, the most dominant and exciting Cub. Next time you go to Wrigley Field, notice the upper deck. Call it "The Seats That Hack Built." The Cubs would have eventually constructed the upper deck, but Wilson's verve and star-power got it built and filled by 1927.

9 If there's a darkest day in Cubs history, it might be May 28, 1930. Pitcher Hal Carlson died in the early morning hours of a stomach hemorrhage. His sudden death unsettled everyone;

only a rainout prevented him from starting a game the previous afternoon.

Carlson's troubles began at the Hotel Carlos, about two blocks north of Wrigley Field. That's where he and a number of Cubs lived during the season. At 2:00 a.m. on May 28, Carlson became ill with stomach cramps. He called clubhouse attendant Eddie Froelich and three of his teammates: Cliff Heathcote, Kiki Cuyler, and Riggs Stephenson. Carlson began bleeding from the mouth. He died at 3:30 a.m., just after the Cubs physician arrived at the hotel.

Carlson suffered from ulcers and other chronic stomach problems, in part from being gassed during World War I. His illness wasn't all that unexpected, but the outcome shocked the team. The Cubs played a game that afternoon and beat the Reds, 6–5. The team held a memorial service that night at Linn's Funeral Home, just a block from the ballpark. They canceled the game the following afternoon, May 29, and a few teammates went to Rockford, Illinois, to attend Carlson's funeral.

Carlson came to the Cubs after 11 years with the Pirates and the Phillies. He was an occasional starter, and had a 4–2 record before his death. In his three and a half years with the Cubs, he went 30–17. The 38-year-old left behind a wife and a three-year-old child. He is the only Cub to die during the season while being on the active roster.

The Hotel Carlos hit the front pages again on July 6, 1932. Violet Popovich shot her lover, Cubs shortstop Billy Jurges, in Room 509. The ballplayer allegedly had ended a relationship with the showgirl. Popovich returned to his room with a gun. When Popovich tried to turn the gun on herself, a fight ensued and Popovich shot Jurges on his right side and his left hand.

The Hotel Carlos evolved into the Sheffield House, a single-room occupancy hotel. It devolved over the years and shut down in 2011, the result of reoccurring code violations and a gentrifying neighborhood. It's an upscale apartment building today, with little recognition (outside of its vintage terra cotta sign) of its most interesting past.

10 The Cubs traded six minor leaguers for hotshot Augie Galan. The switch-hitting infielder paced the 1933 Pacific Coast League with a .356 batting average. Galan got into 66 games on the 1934 Cubs and hit an unexceptional .260. He moved to left field in 1935, batted .314, and led the league in runs and stolen bases.

In 1935, major leaguers slapped into 2,700 double plays. Galan established a record when he didn't bounce into a single one of them. But he had the audacity to hit into one of the two triple plays that year.[18]

Galan started the 1936 All-Star Game at Braves Field in Boston. He smacked a fifth-inning drive off the right field foul pole, the first All-Star Game home run by a Chicago Cub. It led to the National League's 4–3 victory, their first win in four tries.

Galan again wrote himself into the record books on June 25, 1937. He stroked a fourth-inning home run batting left-handed, and an eighth-inning homer batting right-handed. That's the first time a major leaguer homered from both sides of the plate in the same game. It's happened five other times in Cubs history: Ellis Burton in 1963 and 1964, Mark Bellhorn twice in 2002, and Dioner Navarro in 2013. Bellhorn hit his August 29, 2002, "both sides of the plate" home runs in the same inning!

One other Galan note—he became one of only seven post–Dead Ball Era Cubs to lead the team in both home runs and stolen bases in the same season: Max Flack in 1921; Augie Galan in 1937; Ernie Banks in 1955 and 1957; Leon Durham in 1981; Ryne Sandberg in 1985, 1990, and 1992; Sammy Sosa in 1993, 1994, 1995, and 1998; and Derrek Lee in 2005.

Max Flack. (Photo Courtesy of the Library of Congress)

11 The early 1940s Cubs drew poorly. They faded from their salad days of 1926–1939, when they finished above .500 each season and attracted more fans than any other National League team. The 1940–1943 Cubs finished below .500 each season and drew innocuously small crowds. So it made sense that few fans attended a cold and wet September 24, 1943, contest against the lowly Phillies. But this crowd was really small—the smallest in Wrigley Field history.

The 314 fans that day saw a rookie's first major-league game. And what a game for Andy Pafko. The new center fielder drove in four runs in a rain-shortened 7–4 Cubs victory.

Pafko grew up in the little town of Boyceville, Wisconsin. He caught on with the Class-D Eau Claire Bears in 1940. The center fielder moved up the minor-league chain and in 1943 reached Los Angeles of the Pacific Coast League. Pafko led the PCL in hitting, and arrived at Wrigley Field for a trial run with the big club. Pafko hit .379 that September and earned a chance to make the 1944 roster.

While many major leaguers served in the armed forces during World War II, Pafko was deferred (he had high blood pressure). His emergence as an All-Star-caliber outfielder during the war years helped the Cubs win the 1945 National League pennant. Andy hit .298 and drove in 110 runs that year. He scored a 4.2 WAR and finished fourth in the National League Most Valuable Player voting behind teammate Phil Cavarretta.

Pafko's impressive play continued after the war. He appeared in four straight All-Star Games beginning in 1947. He contributed big WAR numbers: 6.0 in 1948, and 6.6 in 1950. Manager Frankie Frisch moved Pafko to third base in 1948. He did well, and befitted his nickname, "Handy Andy." Cubs fans loved the accomplished Pafko; he did little wrong in their eyes.

The Cubs infuriated these same fans when they traded Pafko to the Dodgers on June 15, 1951. Pafko left with Johnny Schmitz, Rube Walker, and Wayne Terwilliger. The Cubs received Gene Hermanski, Joe Hatten, Bruce Edwards, and Eddie Miksis. The Cubs traded their best and most popular player, and outside of Miksis, received little in return. Such was the ineptitude of the 1950s Cubs.

Pafko helped fuel the Dodgers to the 1952 National League pennant. He played in the World Series twice more: in 1957 and 1958 with his home-state Milwaukee Braves. Pafko settled in the Chicago suburbs after retirement. He occasionally traveled down to Wrigley Field, and was celebrated there as one of the last and favorite links to the Cubs' wartime pennant.

12 This is a tricky question. The Indians and Yankees sewed the first numbers on the backs of major-league uniforms in 1929. The rest of the American League added them in 1931, the National League in 1932. That means many Hall of Fame Cubs played their entire careers without uniform numbers, including Cap Anson, John Clarkson, Mordecai Brown, Grover Cleveland Alexander, and Tinker, Evers, and Chance.

In the early days of uniform numbers, players changed numbers often. Billy Herman wore numbers 2 and 4. Gabby Hartnett wore 2, 7, and 9. Charlie Root wore 12, 14, 17, 19, and 49.[19]

Another example of changed numbers played out on September 10, 1933. Newspapers sold scorecards outside Wrigley Field for less than the team sold their own inside. To render the newspaper scorecards worthless, players frequently switched uniform numbers. The team even buttoned new numbers over the old. During the game that day, Kiki Cuyler's number fell off, revealing Charlie Root's number in the official scorecard.

Here are the most common uniform numbers of Cubs who eventually entered the Hall of Fame.

- Number 2—Billy Herman (1932–1936), Gabby Hartnett (1937–1940), Leo Durocher (1966–1972)
- Number 4—Billy Herman (1937–1941), Ralph Kiner (1953–1954), Billy Williams (1959)*
- Number 42—Kiki Cuyler (1943 coach), Lou Boudreau (1960 manager), Tony La Russa (1973),** and Bruce Sutter (1976–1980). Major League Baseball permanently retired number 42 in 1997 to honor Jackie Robinson's 50th anniversary of breaking the modern color barrier.

* Billy Williams wore number 4 during his 18-game call-up in 1959. When he returned to the Cubs in 1960, coaches Charlie Root and Vedie Himsl shared the number that season, so Billy

got number 41. He took number 26 in 1961 and kept it for the rest of his Cubs career.

** Yes, it's *that* Tony La Russa. He appeared just once in a Cubs uniform, on April 6, 1973, Opening Day at Wrigley Field. La Russa pinch-ran for Ron Santo in the ninth inning. He scored the winning run on Rick Monday's bases-loaded walk.

13 The Cubs greatest-hitting pitcher isn't on the list. The 6'5", 275-pound Carlos Zambrano clubbed 23 home runs in his Cubs career. He stroked six home runs alone in 2006, and four in both 2008 and 2009. But he never hit two home runs in a game.

Here's the list of Cubs pitchers who stung two home runs in one game:

Tony Kaufmann	7/4/25 vs. Cardinals	9–1 complete game win
Bill Lee*	5/7/41 at Phillies	11–2 complete game win
Don Cardwell**	9/2/60 at Cardinals	10–4 complete game win
Glen Hobbie***	7/2/61 vs. Cardinals	10–9 win
Fergie Jenkins****	9/1/71 vs. Expos	5–2 complete game win

* Bill Lee hit just five home runs in 1,098 plate appearances. But he cranked two of them in one game.

** Don Cardwell arguably stroked the longest and most interesting home run of any Cubs pitcher. On June 29, 1961, Cardwell jacked one that landed in a yellow convertible parked on Kenmore Avenue, nearly 20 feet north of Waveland Avenue. Caldwell hit 15 major-league home runs.

*** Glen Hobbie smoked his two home runs off Al Cicotte, the great-nephew of the "Black Sox" pitcher Eddie Cicotte.

****Fergie Jenkins hit 13 major-league home runs, all with the Cubs. Jenkins smacked six in 1971 in just 115 at-bats.

One of the Cubs' best-hitting pitchers in recent years, Travis Wood ripped the last grand slam by a Cubs pitcher, against the White Sox on May 30, 2013. Wood also became one of only two relief pitchers to homer in a postseason game. He did that in Game 2 of the National League Division Series against the Giants on October 8, 2016.

"Big" Bill Lee—a great pitcher throughout his career. A great batter on May 7, 1941. (National Baseball Hall of Fame Library, Cooperstown, NY)

14 Through 2016, 119 ballplayers have homered in their first major-league at-bat. These are the eight Cubs who turned the trick.

• Paul Gillespie   September 11, 1942

Paul Gillespie was an unusual catcher: 6'3" and a left-handed batter. He played during World War II and saw the most action in 1945, when the Cubs three best catchers—Clyde McCullough, Bob Scheffing, and Mickey Livingston—all spent time in the military.

Gillespie homered off the Giants' Harry Feldman at the Polo Grounds. On September 29, 1945, he became the first of two major leaguers to homer in both their first and last regular season at-bats. Gillespie played in the 1945 World Series. He started Game 2 and pinch-hit twice, but went 0-for-6.

- Frank Ernaga   May 24, 1957

Cub fans expected great things from the 26-year-old Ernaga, at least for a couple of days. He homered in his first at-bat against Warren Spahn. Then he drilled a triple off Spahn. Ernaga homered and doubled two days later to help the Cubs sweep the Braves at Wrigley Field. But he never cracked the starting lineup (Ernaga got 43 at-bats in two seasons). Ernaga stung minor-league pitching; he stroked 122 home runs in seven seasons.

- Cuno Barragan   September 1, 1961

Facundo Anthony Barragan rattled a home run off the Giants' Dick LeMay at Wrigley Field. Barragan batted 162 more times but never hit another home run. He's one of only ten position players to homer in his first at-bat and never homer again.

The Cubs traded Barragan and Jim Brewer to the Dodgers in 1963. The Cubs received Dick Scott, who pitched just four innings in 1964. While Barragan never played major-league baseball again, Brewer pitched 12 years for the Dodgers and two more with the Angels.

- Carmelo Martinez   August 22, 1983

After walking in the third inning, Martinez homered off the Reds' Frank Pastore in the fifth (walks are not counted as at-bats). On September 4 Martinez hit a three-run pinch-hit home run to key a 9–7 win. For his fifth home run in less than two weeks, Martinez answered a Wrigley Field curtain call.

But the love affair was short-lived. On December 7, 1983, the Cubs traded Martinez, Craig Lefferts, and Fritzie Connally to San Diego in a three-team deal that netted pitcher Scott Sanderson. Martinez and Lefferts played key roles in the Padres' 1984 National League West title. Lefferts won two of the Padres' three National League Championship Series victories against the Cubs.

- Jim Bullinger   June 8, 1992

The only pitcher on the list, Bullinger spent 10 years in the organization, six with the Cubs. He started 63 Cubs games and compiled a 27–28 record and a 1.462 WHIP. Bullinger spent his final two big-league seasons with the Expos and Mariners and went 34–41 for his career.

Bullinger's first major-league at-bat came during his fourth relief appearance. He corked a first-pitch home run off the Cardinals' Rheal Cormier, one of only 31 major-league players to homer on the first pitch. Bullinger's clout helped the Cubs win the first game of a doubleheader. He earned his first major-league save in the nightcap.

- Starlin Castro   May 7, 2010

When the Cubs promoted the 20-year-old Castro from their Double-A Tennessee farm team, he became the first major-league player born in the 1990s. In the second inning at Great American Ballpark, Castro slammed a three-run home run off the Reds' Homer Bailey. He clipped a bases-loaded triple to center in the fifth. Castro's six RBIs that night set a major-league first-game record. His heroics led to a 14–7 win.

- Jorge Soler   August 27, 2014

The Cubs saw Soler's potential and signed the 20-year-old native Cuban to a $30 million contract in June 2012. He worked his way through the system and joined the team in Cincinnati on August 27. Soler homered off Mat Latos in the second inning. Soler hit .292/.330/.573 in 2014. He came alive in the 2015 postseason. He hit .474 and hammered three home runs.

- Willson Contreras   June 19, 2016

Originally signed as a third baseman, the native Venezuelan blossomed once he switched to catcher. Cubs fans knew his potential and when he pinch-hit for Kyle Hendricks, he received a standing ovation. Contreras promptly hit a laser beyond the center field wall. He joined Jim Bullinger as the only "first pitch" home-run hitters in Cubs history. Anthony Rizzo, Kris Bryant, Javier Baez, and Addison Russell also went deep in the Cubs 10–5 win over the Pirates. No major-league team had that kind of a young murderers' row.

15 It's Cubs killers Part II. Some players just have the Cubs' number.

One notorious Cubs killer grew up a Cubs fan in Peru, Illinois. And he even started his career with the team. Russ "The Mad Monk" Meyer pitched just over two years in Chicago and held his own on bad Cubs teams, going 13–12. On October 11, 1948, the Cubs sold Meyer to the Phillies for $20,000.

Meyer started beating the Cubs with regularity in 1949. As a Phillie, he went 3–1, 1–1, 2–0, and 3–0 against the Cubs through the 1952 season. Traded to the Dodgers as part of a four-team deal in early 1953, he beat the Cubs even more, going 5–0, 6–0, and 3–1 against his childhood heroes. That's 23–3 over a seven-year period. It's true that Meyer went from a bad team to good ones—the Phillies won the National League pennant in 1950, and the Dodgers won in 1953 and 1955. Yet Meyer's mastery over his former team surprised everyone, especially the Cubs.

The Cubs tried to stop the agony and brought Meyer back to the North Side before the 1956 season. The team received Meyer, infielder Don Hoak, and slugger Walt Moryn from the Dodgers for relief pitcher Don Elston and outfielder Randy Jackson. The trade ended up a near wash, but Meyer continued to hurt the Cubs in a whole different way. He went just 1–6 in 1956, and the Cubs waived him after the season. Meyer called it quits in 1959 with a 94–73 career record. That's just 71–70 if you subtract his stellar record against the Cubs.

And how did Meyer get his nickname? He and his high school basketball teammates shaved their heads before a big game. The name stuck throughout his professional career.

16 It's odd and a little disconcerting that someone played for both the beloved baseball Cubs and the hated football Packers. It happened. But the circumstance of how it happened makes it plausible.

Cliff Aberson attended Chicago's Senn High School, just a short streetcar ride up Clark Street from Wrigley Field. He starred in both baseball and football. When Aberson graduated in 1940, the Cubs signed the 6'0", 200-pound outfielder to a contract. Aberson spent 1941 and 1942 in Janesville of the Class-D Wisconsin State League.

The military drafted Aberson in 1943 and steered him to football. He played halfback on a service team and caught the eye of a coach who recommended him to the Packers' Curly Lambeau. After his military discharge in April 1946, the Packers signed Aberson to a football contract. He played 10 games for the 1946 Packers and even started in the backfield on November 3 when they lost to the Bears, 10–7 at Wrigley Field. For the season, Aberson gained 161 yards on 48 carries.[20]

Aberson told the Cubs he'd play baseball until August 1, 1947, when he'd report to the Packers. The Cubs assigned him to Class-A Des Moines of the Western League. Aberson ripped the league apart, hit .307, and in July the Cubs promoted him to the big club. Aberson played 47 games on the North Side and hit .279/.369./450. He forgot about football for a while.

Aberson spent most of 1948 with Los Angeles of the Pacific Coast League. He cracked 34 home runs with a 1.111 OPS, but hit a pedestrian .188 in 12 games with the Cubs. Aberson stayed in Los Angeles for most of the 1949 season, and his OPS dropped to .803. He went hitless in only seven at-bats with the Cubs. Aberson never got another shot at the major leagues.

Aberson tried one last time to stick with a major-league sports team. He auditioned for the Second City's other football team, the Chicago Cardinals, in 1950. He didn't make it. His sports career ended with just small sips of glory.

Cliff Aberson lived a life many of us wish for: honorably serving his country, and playing both NFL football and major-league baseball. But Aberson's life is also a cautionary tale—take nothing for granted. Even great things can disappear quickly.

17 Philip Knight Wrigley (P. K.) took over the Cubs after his father's death in 1932. While William Wrigley Jr. earned his reputation as an outgoing, magnanimous, and wholly logical man, son P. K. came across as reserved in his relationships, guarded in his emotions, and measured in fits of forward thinking. He was complex, hard to read, and frustrating to many who knew him. Depending on your perspective, P. K. Wrigley was an inventive thinker, or perhaps someone clueless on how to run a baseball organization.

In January 1963, Wrigley hired Robert Whitlow to be the first "athletic director" of a major-league baseball team. Whitlow was an Air Force colonel who previously held the athletic director position at the Air Force Academy. He came on to control the on-field developments of the Cubs organization.

Wrigley hired Whitlow as athletic director two years after instituting his "College of Coaches" idea. Instead of one man leading the Cubs at each developmental level, the "College" assigned eight coaches who rotated in and out of the major and minor leagues. The goal was a consistent direction throughout. The College of Coaches, however, generated more inconsistencies than it solved. While one coach instructed a player to do something one way, another told him to do it differently. Whitlow arrived to set the system on an even course, to produce a singular way of thought.

Even after Whitlow took the helm, the College still bred confusion. The unusual setup never worked as intended. Whitlow left in frustration before the 1965 season and the Cubs fully abandoned the College of Coaches plan when they hired pugnacious Leo Durocher as full-time manager in 1966. Now everyone knew who was in charge, at least at the major-league level.

Wrigley hired Coleman Griffith in 1937 as Major League Baseball's first sports psychologist. Griffith studied players and proposed ways to improve their mental approach to the game. He recommended repetition in players' thinking and training. He suggested the team replicate game situations in practices to make Cubs players more mentally ready for competition. Managers Charlie Grimm and Gabby Hartnett unfortunately dismissed Griffith outright, and his ideas were never implemented.[21]

P. K. Wrigley sprouted other intriguing ideas over the years. He introduced an early version of an escalator in Wrigley Field. He brought the first organ into a major-league ballpark, and he offered to invest his players' salaries to provide for a secure retirement.

So after roving coaches, an athletic director, and a psychologist, what's the verdict on P. K. Wrigley and his out-of-the-box ideas? His College of Coaches plan is still ridiculed and universally thought to have stunted the organization's development throughout the 1960s. Robert Whitlow served two unsuccessful years as major league baseball's only athletic director. But sports psychology is now essential and commonplace. Every professional and major college sports program uses it to guide an athlete's success. Escalators? They're in virtually every new ballpark. So call Wrigley eccentric and a little out of touch. But in some areas he was ahead of his time.

18 Win Probability Added (WPA) measures the collective winning percentage of each play in a baseball game. A team's chances of winning the game fluctuate depending on a play's outcome. An out lowers your team's chance of winning. A hit raises it. Game-tying hits raise it significantly. Walkoffs rocket it to 100 percent. A high single-game WPA means you did a lot offensively to make your team win that game.

The Cub with the greatest single-game WPA was not a Hall of Famer. He wasn't even a perennial All-Star. He was Jim Hickman. Against the Pirates on May 28, 1970, Hickman singled in the fourth inning to advance a runner who eventually scored. With the Cubs down two runs in the seventh, he tied the game with a two-run home run. With the Cubs down by one in the ninth, Hickman scorched a two-run, game-winning blast off Gene Garber. Hickman's WPA that day tallied 1.181, the eighth highest WPA score in major-league history.

Hickman joined the Cubs in April 1968. The team sent outfielder Ted Savage and minor-league pitcher Jim Ellis to the Dodgers for journeyman Hickman and reliever Phil Regan. The trade helped the Cubs immensely. Regan became the team's top reliever, and Hickman provided power off the bench.

Hickman found his niche with the Cubs. He socked 21 home runs in 1969, highlighted by a June 22 ninth-inning walkoff jack against the Expos. The nine-year veteran produced a MVP-type slash line in 1970: 315/.419/.582. He stroked 32 home runs and drove in 115 RBIs. Hickman finished ninth in the National League in offensive WAR (5.6) and third in OPS (1.001).

His inspired play earned him an All-Star Game appearance, and Hickman participated in one of the more famous plays in All-Star Game history. On July 12 at Riverfront Stadium, Hickman came to bat in the 12th inning of a 4–4 ballgame. With two outs and runners on first and second, he singled to center field. Outfielder Amos Otis caught the ball on a hop and threw home, with catcher Ray Fosse and runner Pete Rose on a collision course at the plate. Rose barreled into Fosse and jarred the ball loose. The National League won the All-Star Game; Fosse dislocated and fractured his shoulder on the play.

Hickman remained with the Cubs through 1973. The Cubs dealt him to the Cardinals after the season as they parted with the remnants of the 1969 team. The Cardinals cut Hickman in July 1974 and he retired to his farm in Tennessee.

Jim Hickman received one vote on the 1980 Hall of Fame ballot. No doubt it came from a Chicago sportswriter who remembered Hickman's renaissance on the Cubs, especially his spectacular 1970 season. "Gentleman Jim" Hickman passed away on June 25, 2016, at 79 years old.

19 The annual baseball draft began in 1965. It came about to level the playing field between the wealthier teams and those too poor to sign high-valued prospects. While it helped to keep teams like the Yankees and the Dodgers from stacking their systems with potential blue-chip studs, the baseball draft was and still remains a real crapshoot with no guarantees; most prospects don't pan out. It's intriguing to evaluate each year's draft. Missed opportunities and diamonds in the proverbial rough abound.

Take the 1967 draft. The Cubs owned the second pick and chose shortstop Terry Hughes. He saw just three at-bats with the North Siders and never developed into a useful major leaguer. Instead of Hughes, the Cubs could have drafted left-handed pitcher Jon Matlack (taken number four by the Mets), catcher Ted Simmons (taken number 10 by the Cardinals), or second baseman Bobby Grich (taken number 19 by the Orioles).

The Cubs held the 12th pick in the 1991 draft and chose outfielder Doug Glanville. He had a middling career (but became a successful baseball commentator). The Indians held the 13th pick, the next one, and chose another outfielder, Manny Ramirez.

The Cubs struck gold in the 2013 draft. They chose second and took Kris Bryant. The third baseman collected both the National League Rookie of the Year Award and the National League Most Valuable Player Award his first two seasons. Bryant compiled a two-year WAR of 13.6. No other player from the 2013 draft (through 2016) compiled a WAR higher than 3.0. And the first pick in the draft, Mark Appel, has already been traded and still pitches in the Phillies' minor league system.

The Cubs owned the first pick in the 1982 draft (in 1981 they finished with the worst record). They chose shortstop Shawon Dunston. The strong-armed Dunston joined the Cubs in 1985 and played 12 years in two stints with the club. Dunston completed a decent Cubs career, with two All-Star Game appearances, 1,119 hits, and a 9.6 WAR.

In that same draft, the Cubs could have chosen Dwight Gooden (taken at number 5). Future Hall of Famers Barry Larkin and Randy Johnson went in the second and fourth rounds. Jose Canseco went in the 15th round and Bret Saberhagen in the 19th. All had much better careers than Dunston.

The draft is speculatively difficult to predict. The Terry Hughes's of the world, the Shawon Dunstons, and the Kris Bryants all look good on paper. But nothing is certain until they get on the field with other professional ballplayers. The draft is baseball on the craps table in Vegas. Winners get Kris Bryant. Losers settle for Terry Hughes.

20 The 2000 Cubs earned their grotesque 65–97 record. Their pitchers sported a frightful 5.25 ERA and a 1.478 WHIP. That's why the 2000 Cubs trotted out 24 pitchers. Ten were left-handed and seven of those were rookies. While their biographies don't sizzle like 100-mph fastballs, they furnish a fascinating look at the state of the team before, during, and after the 2000 season.

Shawon Dunston—first pick in the 1982 amateur draft. (National Baseball Hall of Fame Library, Cooperstown, NY)

Mark Guthrie—The Cubs traded closer Rod Beck to the Red Sox in 1999 for the 11-year veteran. Guthrie pitched 19 games in 2000 before going to the Devil Rays for Dave Martinez. He rejoined the Cubs in 2003 and lost Game 1 of the National League Championship Series, giving up an 11th-inning home run. Guthrie appeared in 765 games during a 15-year career.

Felix Heredia—The native Dominican pitched with the Cubs from 1998 to 2001 and posted a 15–6 record, a 5.01 ERA, and a 1.506 WHIP. He led the 2000 Cubs with 74 appearances. In December 2001, the Cubs traded Heredia to the Blue Jays for Alex Gonzalez.

Andrew Lorraine—He came to the Cubs in 1999 and posted a two-year 3–7 record. Lorraine appeared in eight games in 2000 before being released on May 21. The definition of a journeyman lefty, Lorraine pitched in 59 games for seven teams from 1994 to 2002.

Scott Downs—Downs played in the Cubs organization twice, finally reaching the big club in 2000 when he started 18 games, going 4–3. The Cubs traded Downs to the Expos on July 31 for outfielder Rondell White. In 2007, he led the American League with 81 appearances. Downs eventually wore the uniforms of the Cubs, Expos, Blue Jays, Angels, Braves, White Sox, and Royals.

Will Ohman—The Cubs took Ohman in the eighth round of the 1998 draft. He came to the big leagues on September 19, 2000, and pitched a scoreless ninth inning at Wrigley Field against the Cardinals. Ohman had two stints with the Cubs (2000–2001, 2005–2007). He appeared in 483 games over 10 years.

Phil Norton—Drafted by the Cubs in the 10th round in 1996, Norton reached the majors in 2000, starting two games. He lost his only decision, giving up four fourth-inning home runs at Dodger Stadium. Norton appeared in four more games with the 2003 Cubs and 86 games with the 2003–2004 Reds.

Daniel Garibay—Garibay won two of his first three decisions, pitching scoreless relief stints in San Francisco on May 27 and against the Brewers on June 30. He appeared in 30 games, starting eight of them. Garibay never pitched in the majors after 2000.

Oswaldo Mairena—The native Nicaraguan appeared in two games with the Cubs. He gave up three runs on September 5 in Colorado, and one run on September 9 against the Astros. He pitched in 31 games with the 2002 Marlins.

Danny Young—He appeared in four of the Cubs' first five games. He lost his only decision, giving up an 11th-inning grand slam on March 30 in the Tokyo Dome (the Cubs and Mets played two games in Japan). The Cubs sent him down on April 6 with a 21.00 ERA, and he never pitched in the major leagues again.

Joey Nation—A second-round draft pick by the Braves in 1997, Nation came to the Cubs in a trade that sent Jose Hernandez and Terry Mulholland to Atlanta. Nation's big-league action consisted of two starts: losing September 23 in St. Louis and again on September 28 against the Phillies. He proved to be a better hitter, smacking two singles in four plate appearances.

21 The Cubs had played 141 Opening Day games through 2016. Their record stands at 75–64–2. In those 141 games, they've scored 16 runs twice. It happened in back-to-back years.

On April 4, 2005, the Cubs rapped out 23 hits and humiliated the Diamondbacks in Phoenix, 16–1. Derrek Lee went 4-for-6 with four RBIs, and Aramis Ramirez went 3-for-4 with a home run. Corey Patterson, Todd Walker, and Jeromy Burnitz also rattled three hits apiece. Starting pitcher Carlos Zambrano didn't get the win since he lasted only 4 2/3 innings. Glendon Rusch took the victory.

On April 3, 2006, the Cubs choked the Reds in Cincinnati, 16–7. The North Siders stroked 18 hits, three each by Juan Pierre, Todd Walker, and Matt Murton. Carlos Zambrano again pitched just 4 2/3 innings and didn't get the win. The victory went to Will Ohman, who pitched 1/3 of an inning of relief.

Twice the Cubs scored 15 runs on Opening Day. The Chicago Orphans traveled to Louisville and manhandled the Colonels, 15–1 on April 14, 1899. It was Louisville's final opener, its last of 18 years in the American Association and the National League. The Colonels owner bought the Pittsburgh Pirates after the season and moved his best players to the Steel City. That ended major-league baseball in Kentucky.

The Cubs scored 15 runs again on March 31, 2003, and crushed the Mets, 15–2 at Shea Stadium. The Boys in Blue notched a five-run inning and two four-run innings. Corey Patterson went 4-for-6 and clubbed two home runs and seven RBIs. Kerry Wood got the win.

The Cubs eight highest-scoring Opening Day games occurred on the road. On April 12, 1965, they scored 10 runs against the Cardinals at Wrigley Field. Ernie Banks slapped a game-tying three-run home run in the 9th inning to tie the game at 10–10. The score ended that way when darkness stopped play after 11 innings. The teams replayed the game on July 11, but all the player statistics from the opener counted.

22 This answer is tricky, but you can make a "ballpark" guess by thinking about it a bit. To get lots of at-bats he needed to bat often each game. So it's a good guess he batted leadoff. That eliminates greats like Heine Zimmerman, Hack Wilson, Ernie Banks, and Ryne Sandberg. He also needed to appear in a lot of games. The National League increased the number of games played from 154 to 162 in 1962. So he probably set the record in 1962 or later. That eliminates earlier leadoff hitters like Jimmy Slagle, Max Flack, Jigger Statz, Woody English, and Stan Hack. We also know he played just one year with the team. This eliminates more recent leadoff batters like Don Kessinger, Ivan DeJesus, Bobby Dernier, and Brian McRae.

There is only one Cub since 1962 who saw a full season as a leadoff hitter but played only one season with the team. That player was Juan Pierre. He came to the Cubs from the Marlins on December 7, 2005, traded for Sergio Mitre, Ricky Nolasco, and Renyel Pinto. Pierre's 699 at-bats in 2006 led the league. He also led the league in hits, bunt hits, infield hits, lowest strikeout percentage, and fielding percentage (he did not commit an error in center field).

Pierre had a good year by any standard, but the Cubs let him go after the season. The team lost 96 games in 2006, and instead of the status quo with Pierre, they signed power hitter Alfonso Soriano. The multitalented Soriano got an eight-year $136 million contract. Pierre signed for far less with the Dodgers.

The 2006 season mimicked Pierre's whole career. He knocked 2,217 hits in 14 years, but switched teams six times. Pierre played solid baseball, but his lack of power (only 18 career home runs) limited his usefulness in a run-scoring era. Pierre would have had more value as a base-stealing, artificial turf–chopping hitter in the 1970s or 1980s.

Pierre played one sound year with the Cubs. But when your team loses 96 games, changes happen.

23 The answer to this question isn't one of the 40-game winners of the 19th century. It's not one of the accomplished Dead Ball Era hurlers. Nor is it one of the contemporary Cubs greats like Fergie Jenkins, Greg Maddux, or Jake Arrieta. This pitcher compiled some superb statistics. But by the twilight of his career, many Cubs fans loathed him. Sometimes brilliant, frequently frustrating—it's Carlos Marmol.

PITCHER	HITS PER NINE INNINGS
Carlos Marmol	5.9
Jake Arrieta	6.2
Orval Overall	6.9
PITCHER	KS PER NINE INNINGS
Carlos Marmol	11.7
Mark Prior	10.4
Kerry Wood	10.3

Carlos Marmol racked up these and other impressive Cubs statistics. He ranks second in games pitched with 483 (behind Charlie Root). He ranks third all-time with 117 saves (behind Lee Smith and Bruce Sutter). He shares the record for consecutive saves in a season (19 in 2012). He holds the team relief record for strikeouts in a season (138 in 2010). Major leaguers hit only .188 against him.

But by the end of his Cubs career, Marmol often shot himself in the foot with walks. The walks expanded batters' .188 average against him to a league-average .332 on-base percentage. In 2012 and 2013, his WHIP ballooned to 1.536 and 1.699 (he compiled a tiny 0.927 WHIP in 2008).

Carlos Marmol pitched spectacularly for five years. Near the end, he pitched gut-wrenchingly hideous. For a player who dominated the opposition as much as he did, Cubs fans were overjoyed to see him dealt to the Dodgers in 2013.

24 We've reached the end of the book, and the end of the alphabet. Are you still on the mound? The fourteen "Z Cubs" appear in chronological order. The dates indicate the seasons played on the North Side.

- Henry "Heinie" Zimmerman   1907–1916

A gifted athlete who played every infield position, Zimmerman had rare power in the Dead Ball Era. He won the National League Triple Crown in 1912 with a .372 average, 14 home runs, and 104 RBIs. But the Cubs tired of his fits and starts of motivation and traded him to the Giants. In New York, he consorted with gamblers, got caught up with "crooked" teammates, and offered players money to throw games. While not convicted of these actions, he never played after the 1919 season.

- George Washington "Zip" Zabel   1913–1915

George Zabel was a rarity among early-20th-century ballplayers: He was college educated and he even continued his studies while playing for the Cubs. Zabel entered the record books on June 17, 1915. He came on in relief in the first inning and pitched 18 1/3 innings, until the Cubs won it in the 19th. That's the longest relief appearance before or since in major-league history.

- Edward "Dutch" Zwilling   1916

Zwilling got 87 at-bats with the 1910 White Sox. He resurfaced with the "outlaw" Chicago Federals in 1914. Zwilling hit more home runs than any Federal League player—29. He joined the

Cubs when Weeghman bought the team in 1916, but played sparingly. Zwilling held one more claim to fame, being the last major-league player alphabetically until Tony Zyth joined the Seattle Mariners in 2015.

- Rollie Zeider   1916–1918

Zeider's career mirrored Zwilling's: a start with the White Sox, a jump to the Chicago Federals, and a switch to the Cubs in 1916 (Zeider and Zwilling are the only men to play for the White Sox, Chi-Feds, and Cubs). Zimmerman, Zwilling, and Zeider all played for the 1916 Cubs, a triple-Z rarity that happened only once more in major-league history (the 1999 Texas Rangers had Jeff Zimmerman, Todd Zeile, and Gregg Zaun).

- Bob Zick   1954

A local boy from Fenger High School and the University of Illinois, Zick made eight appearances for the Cubs and ground out an 8.27 ERA in 16 1/3 innings. Zick is remembered best from this often repeated story—when he reported to spring training in 1954 he told Cubs manager Stan Hack, "I'm Zick." Hack replied, "I'm not feeling so well myself."

- Don Zimmer   1960–1961

Zimmer spent six years with the Dodgers before coming to the Cubs in April 1960. He hit 13 home runs in 1961 and played in the July 11 All-Star Game. The Mets chose Zimmer in the 1962 Expansion Draft. He managed the Cubs from 1988 to 1991, and he led the 1989 "Boys of Zimmer" to the National League East title. Zimmer managed 13 seasons in the major leagues and worked in the game for over 65 years. He died at the age of 83 on June 4, 2014.

- Oscar Zamora   1974–1976

The native Cuban right-hander led the team in games (56) and saves (10) in 1974. After the 1977 season, the Astros chose Zamora in the reentry draft. In 148 games for the Cubs, he went 13–14 with a 4.34 ERA.

- Geoff Zahn   1975–1976

Zahn came to the Cubs in the 1975 Burt Hooton trade. He went 2–8 in two seasons and was released. Zahn resurrected his career and went 105–95 in nine seasons with the Twins and the Angels. He finished sixth for the 1982 American League Cy Young Award. He managed the University of Michigan baseball team from 1996 to 2001.

- Eddie Zambrano   1993–1994

Zambrano (no relation to Carlos) toiled nine years in the minor leagues before getting a chance on the Cubs. The outfielder performed well in 1993 at Triple-A Iowa, hitting .303 and slugging 32 home runs. In 1994 with the Cubs, he stroked six home runs and posted an .828 OPS. Zambrano ended up in the Red Sox organization but never played again in the major leagues.

- Todd Zeile   1995

Third baseman Zeile played seven seasons with the Cardinals before coming to the Cubs on June 16, 1995. In 299 at-bats, he hit just .227 and left as a free agent following the season. Zeile played for nine teams during nine more major-league seasons, ending his career in 2004 with 2,004 hits. Zeile owns one exhausting major-league record. He's the only man to hit a home run for more than 10 different teams.

- Julio Zuleta   2000–2001

The 6'6" native Panamanian showed promise, but after eight years in the minors the Cubs ran out of patience. In 68 at-bats in 2000, he hit eight doubles with an .887 OPS. Zuleta stumbled in 2001 and hit only .217. He fled to Japan and starred there for six years, slugging 150 home runs.

- Carlos Zambrano   2001–2011

A major talent who commanded a variety of pitches, the Venezuelan Zambrano spent 11 years with the Cubs and compiled a 125–81 record. On September 14, 2008, he no-hit the Astros. But late in his career, the Cubs suspended Zambrano three times for anger issues. He was out of the big leagues just past his 31st birthday.

- Ben Zobrist   2016

Zobrist spent his first nine with the Rays. The switch-hitter split 2015 with the A's and the Royals and helped the latter win the World Series. The Eureka, Illinois, native signed a four-year contract with the Cubs before the 2016 season. He won the 2016 World Series Most Valuable Player Award.

- Rob Zastryzny   2016

A second-round draft pick in 2013, the Canadian-born Zas-tryzny appeared in eight games in 2016 and compiled a 1–0 record and a 1.13 ERA. He holds the distinction of being the first drafted pitcher in the Theo Epstein era to make the Cubs roster.

Heinie Zimmerman—Dead Ball Era superstar. (National Baseball Hall of Fame Library, Cooperstown, NY)

5

POSTSCRIPT

I did not attend any of the 2016 World Series games. But the morning after Game 7, I drove to Chicago. I headed straight to the corner of Clark and Addison Streets and spent four hours under the famed Wrigley Field marquee. I wasn't alone. Thousands of Cubs fans joined me that afternoon. Fans of all stripes made the pilgrimage to take a photograph or a selfie in front of the vintage marquee that proclaimed the seemingly impossible words, "World Series Champions."

Families came, sometimes multiple generations with a grandparent, child, and grandchild. Parents snapped photos with their children, there to prove to later generations that they were alive when the Cubs won a championship. One man held a framed photograph of his father. His dad, a longtime Cubs fan, left the earth before he experienced what his son savored to no end the night before. The son didn't smile for the photo, but revealed a triumphant and satisfied look. He and his father shared this moment together.

Couples hugged and kissed. Children held up "W" flags. Dogs dressed in Cubs T-shirts periodically wandered by led by adults in similar garb.

Sounds reverberated outside the old ballpark. Car horns jubilantly blasted, helicopters whirred. One fan wept out loud. People entered conversations with strangers and laughed. They said "excuse me" when they jockeyed for the best location to shoot their precious image.

On the afternoon of November 3, 2016, the corner of Clark and Addison, specifically the sidewalk under the Wrigley Field marquee, must have been the happiest corner in America. These Cubs fans arrived to seek tangible proof that the previous night was real, that it wasn't a dream. Most Cubs fans had that dream before, a beautiful one where their sartorial blue-pinstriped heroes captured the World Series. But on November 2, 2016, it actually happened.

Thousands came to Wrigley Field that day. Millions attended the victory parade and rally. On the other side of the ballpark, fans drew lovely images and notes in chalk to commemorate, remember, and share this glorious event.

Cubs fans will never forget that victory. I'll never forget that afternoon.

Magnificent—the marquee proclaims the long-awaited World Series victory. (Author's collection)

Endnotes

1. "Winds over Wrigley Field," *Chicago Tribune*, August 5, 2001.
2. Jon Greenberg, "Heart on Sleeve, Piniella Says Goodbye," *Chicago Cubs Report*, www.espn.com/chicago/mlb/columns/story?id=5485400&columnist==greenberg_jon, August 23, 2010.
3. Scott Miller, "Inside the Chicago Cubs' Hiring of Joe Maddon, One of MLB's Best Managers," http://bleacherreport.com/articles/2297391-inside-the-chicago-cubs-theft-of-joe-maddon-one-of-mlbs-best-managers, December 15, 2014.
4. Paul Sullivan, "Sitting on a Goldmine," *Chicago Tribune*, July 6, 2014.
5. Scott Miller, "Rain Delay Speech Helps End Drought as Chicago Cubs Win Historic World Series," http://bleacherreport.com/articles/2673738-rain-delay-speech-helps-end-drought-as-chicago-cubs-win-historic-world-series, November 3, 2016.
6. "Gabby Hartnett," Baseballhall.org/hof/Hartnett-gabby.
7. Jerome Holtzman, "The Cubs All-Time Best," *Chicago Tribune*, February 14, 1989.
8. Eddie Gold and Art Ahrens, *The Golden Era Cubs* (Chicago: Bonus Books, 1985), 116.
9. William Leonard, "A City Landmark—Billy Goat," *Chicago Tribune*, December 26, 1967.
10. Don McLeese, "Are Day Games Killing the Cubs?," *Chicago Sports*, May/June 1980: 24–28.
11. Michael Clair, "Ozzy Osbourne Once Led 'Take Me Out to the Ballgame' at Wrigley Field, and It Was Not Great," *Cut 4*. http://m.mlb.com/cutfour/2015/08/17/143328266/ozzy-osbourne-once-forgot-lyrics-while-at-cubs-wrigley-field.
12. Fay Young, "Through the Years," *Chicago Defender*, April 19, 1947.

13. Dick Rosen, "Peanuts Lowrey," http://sabr.org/bioproj/person/fae7f0da.
14. Joseph Gerard, "Mike Gonzalez," http://sabr.org/bioproj/person/75c3d9b1.
15. Andrew Dolphin, "No Bang off the Bench? A Closer Look at Pinch Hitting," http://www.baseballprospectus.com/article.php?articleid=5404, August 9, 2006.
16. "Larry Corcoran," https://en.wikipedia.org/wiki/Larry Corcoran.
17. "Donovan Weakens and Chicago Wins," *New York Times*, October 12, 1908.
18. Kevin Graham, "Augie Galan—Double Trouble? Or Triple Threat?," https://baseballrevisited.wordpress.com/2012/02/01/augie-galan-double-trouble-or-triple-threat, February 1, 2012.
19. Al Yellon, Kasey Ignarski, and Matthew Silverman, *Cubs by the Numbers* (New York: Skyhorse Publishing, Inc., 2009).
20. Gary Bedingfield, "Cliff Aberson," *Baseball in Wartime*, www.baseballinwartime.com/player_biographies/aberson_cliff.htm.
21. Christopher D. Green, "America's First Sports Psychologist," *Monitor on Psychology*, Vol. 43, No. 4, www.apa.org/monitor/2012/04/sports.aspx.

Bibliography

Ahrens, Arthur. "The Tragic Saga of Charlie Hollocher." http://research.sabr.org/journals/the-tragic-saga-of-charlei-hollocher.

Bales, Jack. "The Shootings of Billy Jurges and Eddie Waitkus." *Wrigleyivy.com*. wrigleyivy.com/the-shootings-of-billy-jurges-and-eddie-waitkus.

Bedingfield, Gary. "Cliff Aberson." *Baseball in Wartime*. www.baseballinwartime.com/player_biographies/aberson_cliff.htm.

Brickhouse, Jack, Jack Rosenberg, and Nick Colletti. *Thanks for Listening!* South Bend, IN: Diamond Communications, Inc., 1986.

Carr, Jason. *2016 Chicago Cubs Media Guide*. Chicago: Chicago Cubs Baseball Club, LLC, 2016.

Clair, Michael. "Ozzy Osbourne Once Led 'Take Me Out to the Ballgame' at Wrigley Field, and It Was Not Great." *Cut 4*. http://m.mlb.com/cutfour/2015/08/17/143328266/ozzy-osbourne-once-forgot-lyrics-while-at-cubs-wrigley-field.

Dolphin, Andrew. "No Bang off the Bench? A Closer Look at Pinch Hitting." http://www.baseballprospectus.com/article.php?articleid=5404, August 9, 2006.

"Donovan Weakens and Chicago Wins." *New York Times*, October 12, 1908.

Fleitz, David L. *Cap Anson: The Grand Old Man of Baseball*. Jefferson, NC: McFarland & Company Inc., 2005.

"Gabby Hartnett." Baseballhall.org/hof/Hartnett-gabby.

Gerard, Joseph. "Mike Gonzalez." http://sabr.org/bioproj/person/75c3d9b1.

Gold, Eddie, and Art Ahrens. *The Golden Era Cubs*. Chicago: Bonus Books, 1985.

Graham, Kevin. "Augie Galan—Double Trouble? Or Triple Threat?" https://baseballrevisited.wordpress.com/2012/02/01/augie-galan-double-trouble-or-triple-threat, February 1, 2012.

Green, Christopher D. Dr. "America's First Sports Psychologist." *Monitor on Psychology*, Vol. 43, No. 4, www.apa.org/monitor/2012/04/sports.aspx.

Greenberg, Jon. "Heart on Sleeve, Piniella Says Goodbye." *Chicago Cubs Report*, www.espn.com/chicago/mlb/columns/story?id=5485400&columnist==greenberg_jon, August 23 , 2010.

Holtzman, Jerome. "The Cubs All-Time Best." *Chicago Tribune*, February 14, 1989.

Kruse, Karen. *A Chicago Firehouse: Stories of Wrigleyville's Engine 78*. Mount Pleasant, SC: Arcadia Publishing, 2001.

"Larry Corcoran." https://en.wikipedia.org/wiki/Larry Corcoran.

Leonard, William. "A City Landmark—Billy Goat." *Chicago Tribune*, December 26, 1967.

McLeese, Don. "Are Day Games Killing the Cubs?" *Chicago Sports*, May/June 1980.

Miller, Scott. "Inside the Chicago Cubs' Hiring of Joe Maddon, One of MLB's Best Managers." http://bleacherreport.com/articles/2297391-inside-the-chicago-cubs-theft-of-joe-maddon-one-of-mlbs-best-managers, December 15, 2014.

Miller, Scott. "Rain Delay Speech Helps End Drought as Chicago Cubs Win Historic World Series." http://bleacherreport.com/articles/2673738-rain-delay-speech-helps-end-drought-as-chicago-cubs-win-historic-world-series, November 3, 2016.

Rosen, Dick. "Peanuts Lowrey." http://sabr.org/bioproj/person/fae7f0da.

Santo, Ron, and Randy Minkoff. *For Love of Ivy*. Chicago: Bonus Books, Inc. 1993.

Sullivan, Paul. "Sitting on a Goldmine." *Chicago Tribune*, July 6, 2014.

Williams, Billy, and Irv Haag. *Billy: The Classic Hitter*. Chicago: Rand McNally & Company, 1974.

Yellon, Al, Kasey Ignarski, and Matthew Silverman. *Cubs by the Numbers.* New York: Skyhorse Publishing, Inc., 2009.

Young, Fay. "Through the Years." *Chicago Defender*, April 19, 1947.

Acknowledgments

Thanks to the staff at two great public libraries: the Columbus Metropolitan Library and the Worthington Public Library. Public libraries are our best and most cost-effective public resources; they should be cherished. Thanks to Niels Aaboe at Sports Publishing for offering the idea. Thanks to my agent, Rita Rosenkrantz, for ironing out the details. And thanks to Kerry for supporting me once again!